Ninja Foodi
2-Basket Air Fryer
Cookbook

Easy & Delicious Air Fry, Dehydrate, Roast, Bake, Reheat, and More Recipes for Beginners and Advanced Users

Helen Bently

Table of Contents

Chapter 5 Poultry Mains Recipes 54

Chapter 6 Beef, Pork, and Lamb Recipes 66

Chapter 7 Dessert Recipes 78

Conclusion 88

Appendix 1 Measurement Conversion Chart 89

Appendix 2 Air Fryer Cooking Chart 90

Appendix 3 Recipes Index 91

Introduction

The Ninja Foodi 2-Basket Air Fryer is a new arrival amongst their wide range of air fryers. This air fryer has 2 independent baskets that let you cook two different food items or bulk of food at the same time with two different or the same settings. It is way different than the traditional air fryer that usually has a single basket.

As by the name, this comprehensive guide is targeted toward all those busy people who want to enjoy some delicious but less fatty meal that tastes delicious and its texture is as crispy as restaurant meals.

So, if you are a housewife or have an on-to-go lifestyle, then this Ninja Foodi is an excellent appliance to fulfill all the cooking needed. Whether it an early morning breakfast, afternoon brunch, or late-night dinner party, now you can create some remarkable restaurant-style meals right in your kitchen.

Take advantage of any of the recipes provided in this cookbook to enjoy a meal that keeps your weight maintained.

The ninja Foodi 2 basket air fryer lets you prepare food that is delicious and offers a hand-free cooking experience with less hustle. This cookbook includes easily prepared meals targeted toward the American audience.

No doubt, the Ninja foodie 2-basket air fryer plays a very important role in making healthy meals. Unlike, any other appliance like a deep fryer and broiler it prepares food in less oil. Now, stop sacrificing the taste and texture and enjoy whatever you liked.

In this cookbook we are covering the following:
• Introduction
• The Functions of Ninja Foodi 2-Basket Air Fryer
• How to Use Ninja Foodi 2 Basket Air Fryer
• Maintaining and Cleaning the Appliance
• 200+ delicious and mouth warring recipes
• 3-week diet plan
• Conclusion

Along with the 80 recipes, we have added beautiful images of the recipes and snippets of the nutritional information, so that that overall calories intake process stays on right track.

What is Ninja Foodi 2-Basket Air Fryer

The new Ninja 2-basket air fryer has a DUAL-ZONE technology that includes a smart finish button that cooks two food items in two different ways at the same time. It has a MATCH button that cooks food by copying the setting across both zones.

The 8 –quart air fryer has a capacity that can cook full family meals up to 4 pounds. The two zones have their separate baskets that cook food using cyclonic fans that heat food rapidly with circulating hot air all-around. The baskets are very easy to clean and dishwasher safe. The ninja Foodi 2-basket air fryer has a range of 105-450 degrees F temperature.

The Ninja foodie 2-basket air fryer is easily available at an affordable price online and at local stores.

If you are always worried about the lack of time to prepare two different meals or a large number of meals in a single go, then this appliance is a must to have.
It can hold plenty of food that can feed a large family.

The Functions of Ninja Foodi 2-Basket Air Fryer

This Ninja foodie 2-Basket Air fryer eliminates the traditional back-to-back cooking by providing ease of two baskets that cook food at the same time.

Its function includes a Smart Finish feature cooking system, so both items of food are cooked at the same time.

This Ninja foodie air fryer surely makes crispy food by removing the moist from the food by circulating the hot air around.

The Ninja® Air Fryer function includes.
• Air Fry
• Air Broil
• Roast
• Bake
• Reheat
• Dehydrate
•
Package Dimensions: 18.3 x 16.3 x 15.7 inches
Item Weight: 24.3 pounds
Manufacturer: Ninja

If you want to end the cooking time of one zone, while using both zones you need to choose the zone you like to stop, and then press the START/STOP to end the cooking process for that specific zone.

When the drawer is removed from the Ninja foodie 2-basket air fryer, the cooking process is automatically stopped.

The TEMP arrows are used to set the desired temperature.

The TIME arrows are used to set the time according to specific needs.

Once cooking is done the "END" appears on the screen.

How to Use Ninja Foodi 2 Basket Air Fryer

The use of Ninja foodie 2-basket air fryer is as easy as a click of a button.

For most of the recipes, it is necessary and recommended to grease the air fryer baskets with oil spray.

You simply add the food to the basket and select the required function to AIR FRY, BROIL, BAKE, roast, and more.

The +and – buttons to adjust the cooking time and temperature control button can be separately used to adjust the cooking time of the food in both zones.

Once the food gets cooked, you can take out the baskets and serve food from both zones of the air fryer to the serving plates.

Some useful button to cook food:

MAX CRISP: It is used to prepare some of the crispest French fries and chicken nuggets. With lesser amount of oil, you can make more crispy food than a traditional fryer.

ROAST: The roast function easily prepares some tender and juicy meat in no time.

REHEAT: The reheat function can easily help you enjoy any leftover food.

DEHYDRATE: Now you can easily dehydrate most of the fruits and the vegetables, and save money you spend to buy a separate dehydrator.

BAKE: This function helps creates delicious dessert and baked treats.

SYNC button: This button can be used when the user wants to finish two different zones with different settings together.

MATCH button: This button automatically matches both the zone time and temperature.

STANDBY MODE: The unit remains with no interaction for more than 10 minutes, it goes to standby mode.

HOLD MODE: This will appear during sync mode, as one zone is cooking and the other is on hold.

Temperature Ranges

- Bake Function:250- 400 Degrees F (Up To 1-½ Hour)
- Roast Function: 250-400 Degrees F (For Up To 4 Hours)
- Reheat Fucniton:270 Degrees F To 400degrees F (1minutes to 1hours)
- Dehydrate Functions: 105 -195 Degrees F (1-12 Hours)
- Air Broil Function400 Degrees F To 450 Degrees F (1 Minutes 30 Minutes)

Maintaining and Cleaning the Appliance

- The Ninja 2-basket air fryer is not intended to be used outdoor.
- It is very important to check the voltage indication are corresponding to the main voltage from the switch.
- Do not immerse the appliance in water.
- Keep the cord away from the hot area.
- Do not touch the outer surface of the air fryer hen using for cooking purposes.
- Put the appliance on a horizontal and flat surface.
- Unplug the appliance after use.

Cleaning
- First, unplug the power cord of the air fryer.
- Make sure the appliance is cooled before cleaning.
- The air fryer should be cleaning after every use.
- To clean the outer surface, use a damp towel.
- Clean the inside of the air fryer with a nonabrasive sponge.
- The accessories of the air fryer are dishwasher safe, but to extend the life of the drawers, it's recommended to wash them manually.

4 Weeks Diet Plan

Week 1

Day 1:
Breakfast: Biscuit Balls
Lunch: Quinoa Patties
Snack: Spicy Chicken Tenders
Dinner: Chinese BBQ Pork
Dessert: Oreo Rolls

Day 2:
Breakfast: Sausage with Eggs
Lunch: Mixed Air Fry Veggies
Snack: Chicken Tenders
Dinner: Chicken Breast Strips
Dessert: Biscuit Doughnuts

Day 3:
Breakfast: Breakfast Bacon
Lunch: Fresh Mix Veggies in Air Fryer
Snack: Mozzarella Sticks
Dinner: Spicy Fish Fillet with Onion Rings
Dessert: Mini Blueberry Pies

Day 4:
Breakfast: Yellow Potatoes with Eggs
Lunch: Green Beans with Baked Potatoes
Snack: Fried Pickles
Dinner: Smoked Salmon
Dessert: Lava Cake

Day 5:
Breakfast: Pumpkin Muffins
Lunch: Cheesy Potatoes with Asparagus
Snack: Crispy Chickpeas
Dinner: Breaded Pork Chops
Dessert: Baked Apples

Day 6:
Breakfast: Sweet Potatoes Hash
Lunch: Garlic Herbed Baked Potatoes
Snack: Mac and Cheese Balls
Dinner: Ham Burger Patties
Dessert: Cinnamon Sugar Dessert Fries

Day 7:
Breakfast: Egg with Baby Spinach
Lunch: Pepper Poppers
Snack: Tater Tots
Dinner: Chicken Leg Piece
Dessert: Apple Fritters

Week 2

Day 1:
Breakfast: Air Fried Sausage
Lunch: Garlic Potato Wedges in Air Fryer
Snack: Blueberries Muffins
Dinner: Chicken Ranch Wraps
Dessert: Mini Strawberry and Cream Pies

Day 2:
Breakfast: Cinnamon Toasts
Lunch: Air Fried Okra
Snack: Strawberries and Walnuts Muffins
Dinner: Steak Fajitas With Onions and Peppers
Dessert: Chocolate Chip Cake

Day 3:
Breakfast: Breakfast Casserole
Lunch: Sweet Potatoes with Honey Butter
Snack: Stuffed Mushrooms
Dinner: Keto Baked Salmon with Pesto
Dessert: Apple Crisp

Day 4:
Breakfast: Breakfast Sausage Omelet
Lunch: Fried Olives
Snack: Zucchini Chips
Dinner: Glazed Steak Recipe
Dessert: Jelly Donuts

Day 5:
Breakfast: Egg and Avocado in The Ninja Foodi
Lunch: Zucchini with Stuffing
Snack: Jalapeño Popper Chicken
Dinner: Chicken Parmesan
Dessert: Air Fried Bananas

Day 6:
Breakfast: Bacon and Egg Omelet
Lunch: Herb and Lemon Cauliflower
Snack: Fried Halloumi Cheese
Dinner: Two-Way Salmon
Dessert: Strawberry Nutella Hand Pies

Day 7:
Breakfast: Banana and Raisins Muffins
Lunch: Stuffed Tomatoes
Snack: Peppered Asparagus
Dinner: Salmon with Coconut
Dessert: Pumpkin Muffins with Cinnamon

Week 3

Day 1:
Breakfast: Bacon and Eggs for Breakfast
Lunch: Fried Asparagus
Snack: Cheddar Quiche
Dinner: Pork Chops
Dessert: Churros

Day 2:
Breakfast: Air Fryer Sausage Patties
Lunch: Fried Avocado Tacos
Snack: Ravioli
Dinner: Yummy Chicken Breasts
Dessert: Fudge Brownies

Day 3:
Breakfast: Hash Browns
Lunch: Buffalo Bites
Snack: Stuffed Bell Peppers
Dinner: Juicy Pork Chops
Dessert: Air Fryer Sweet Twists

Day 4:
Breakfast: Donuts
Lunch: Brussels Sprouts
Snack: Grill Cheese Sandwich
Dinner: Salmon with Broccoli and Cheese
Dessert: Mini Blueberry Pies

Day 5:
Breakfast: Banana Muffins
Lunch: Air Fried Okra
Snack: Blueberries Muffins
Dinner: Korean BBQ Beef
Dessert: Mini Strawberry and Cream Pies

Day 6:
Breakfast: Sausage with Eggs
Lunch: Sweet Potatoes with Honey Butter
Snack: Spicy Chicken Tenders
Dinner: Paprika Pork Chops
Dessert: Oreo Rolls

Day 7:
Breakfast: Breakfast Bacon
Lunch: Quinoa Patties
Snack: Mozzarella Sticks
Dinner: Beef & Broccoli
Dessert: Biscuit Doughnuts

Week 4

Day 1:
Breakfast: Air Fried Bacon and Eggs
Lunch: Mushroom Roll-Ups
Snack: Parmesan Crush Chicken
Dinner: Glazed Thighs with French Fries
Dessert: Grilled Peaches

Day 2:
Breakfast: Egg White Muffins
Lunch: Kale and Spinach Chips
Snack: Sweet Bites
Dinner: Honey Sriracha Mahi Mahi
Dessert: Fried Oreos

Day 3:
Breakfast: Perfect Cinnamon Toast
Lunch: Garlic-Rosemary Brussels Sprouts
Snack: Garlic Bread
Dinner: Spicy Chicken
Dessert: Lemony Sweet Twists

Day 4:
Breakfast: Bagels
Lunch: Beets With Orange Gremolata and Goat's Cheese
Snack: Dijon Cheese Sandwich
Dinner: Seafood Shrimp Omelet
Dessert: Apple Crisp

Day 5:
Breakfast: Air Fried Sausage
Lunch: Fresh Mix Veggies in Air Fryer
Snack: Chicken Tenders
Dinner: Codfish with Herb Vinaigrette
Dessert: Chocolate Chip Cake

Day 6:
Breakfast: Cinnamon Toasts
Lunch: Fried Olives
Snack: Strawberries and Walnuts Muffins
Dinner: Cornish Hen with Baked Potatoes
Dessert: Chocolate Chip Muffins

Day 7:
Breakfast: Breakfast Casserole
Lunch: Garlic Potato Wedges in Air Fryer
Snack: Cauliflower Gnocchi
Dinner: Fish and Chips
Dessert: Bread Pudding

Chapter 1 Breakfast Recipes

Sausage with Eggs

Prep Time: 10 Minutes
Cook Time: 13 Minutes
Serves: 2
Ingredients:
• 4 sausage links, raw and uncooked
• 4 eggs, uncooked
• 1 tablespoon green onion
• 2 tablespoons chopped tomatoes
• Salt and black pepper, to taste
• 2 tablespoons milk, dairy
• Oil spray, for greasing
Preparation:
1. Take a bowl and whisk eggs in it.
2. Then pour milk, and add the onions and tomatoes.
3. Whisk it all well.
4. Now season it with salt and black pepper.
5. Take one cake pan that fits inside the air fryer and grease it with oil spray.
6. Pour the omelet into the greased cake pan.
7. Put the cake pan inside zone 1 of the Ninja Foodie 2-Basket Air Fryer.
8. Now place the sausage link into the zone 2 basket.
9. Select BAKE for zone 1 basket and set the timer to 8-10 minutes at 300 degrees F.
10. For zone 2, select the AIR FRY button and set the timer to 12 minutes at 390 degrees F.
11. Once the cooking cycle is complete, serve by transferring it to plates.
12. Chop the sausage or cut it in round chunks and then mix it with the egg.
13. Enjoy hot as a delicious breakfast.
Serving Suggestion: Serve it with toasted bread slices
Variation Tip: Use almond milk if you like non-dairy milk
Nutritional Information Per Serving:
Calories 240 | Fat 18.4g| Sodium 396mg | Carbs 2.8g | Fiber 0.2g | Sugar 2g | Protein 15.6g

Yellow Potatoes with Eggs

Prep Time: 10 Minutes
Cook Time: 35 Minutes
Serves: 2
Ingredients:
• 1 pound of Dutch yellow potatoes, quartered
• 1 red bell pepper, chopped
• Salt and black pepper, to taste
• 1 green bell pepper, chopped
• 2 teaspoons olive oil
• 2 teaspoons garlic powder
• 1 teaspoon onion powder
• 1 egg
• ¼ teaspoon butter
Preparation:
1. Toss together diced potatoes, green pepper, red pepper, salt, black pepper, and olive oil along with garlic powder and onion powder.
2. Put the potatoes in the zone 1 basket of the air fryer.
3. Take a ramekin and grease it with oil spray.
4. Whisk the egg in a bowl and add salt and pepper along with ½ teaspoon of butter.
5. Pour the egg into the ramekin and place it in the zone 2 basket.
6. Set the timer for zone 1 basket to 30-35 minutes at 400 degrees F at AIR FRY mode.
7. Now for zone 2, set it to AIR FRY mode at 350 degrees F for 8-10 minutes.
8. Press the Sync button and press START/STOP button so both will finish at the same time.
9. Once done, serve and enjoy.
Serving Suggestion: Serve it with sourdough toasted bread slices
Variation Tip: Use white potatoes instead of yellow Dutch potatoes
Nutritional Information Per Serving:
Calories 252 | Fat 7.5g | Sodium 37mg | Carbs 40g | Fiber 3.9g | Sugar 7g | Protein 6.7g

Biscuit Balls

Prep Time: 10 minutes.
Cook Time: 18 minutes.
Serves: 6
Ingredients:
• 1 tablespoon butter
• 2 eggs, beaten
• ¼ teaspoon pepper
• 1 can (10.2-oz) Pillsbury Buttermilk biscuits
• 2 ounces cheddar cheese, diced into ten cubes
• Cooking spray
• Egg Wash
• 1 egg
• 1 tablespoon water
Preparation:
1. Place a suitable non-stick skillet over medium-high heat and cook the bacon until crispy, then place it on a plate lined with a paper towel.
2. Melt butter in the same skillet over medium heat. Beat eggs with pepper in a bowl and pour them into the skillet.
3. Stir cook for 5 minutes, then remove it from the heat.
4. Add bacon and mix well.
5. Divide the dough into 5 biscuits and slice each into 2 layers.
6. Press each biscuit into 4-inch round.
7. Add a tablespoon of the egg mixture at the center of each round and top it with a piece of cheese.
8. Carefully fold the biscuit dough around the filling and pinch the edges to seal.
9. Whisk egg with water in a small bowl and brush the egg wash over the biscuits.
10. Place half of the biscuit bombs in each of the crisper plate and spray them with cooking oil.
11. Return the crisper plate to the Ninja Foodi Dual Zone Air Fryer.
12. Choose the Air Fry mode for Zone 1 and set the temperature to 375 degrees F and the time to 14 minutes.
13. Select the "MATCH" button to copy the settings for Zone 2.
14. Initiate cooking by pressing the START/STOP button.
15. Flip the egg bombs when cooked halfway through, then resume cooking.
16. Serve warm.
Serving Suggestion: Serve the eggs balls with crispy bacon.
Variation Tip: Add dried herbs to the egg filling.
Nutritional Information Per Serving:
Calories 102 | Fat 7.6g |Sodium 545mg | Carbs 1.5g | Fiber 0.4g | Sugar 0.7g | Protein 7.1g
Carbs 20g | Fiber 0.6g | Sugar 3.3g | Protein 16g

Breakfast Sausage Omelet

Prep Time: 10 Minutes
Cook Time: 8 Minutes
Serves: 2
Ingredients:
• ¼ pound breakfast sausage, cooked and crumbled
• 4 eggs, beaten
• ½ cup pepper Jack cheese blend
• 2 tablespoons green bell pepper, sliced
• 1 green onion, chopped
• 1 pinch cayenne pepper
• Cooking spray
Preparation:
1. Take a bowl and whisk eggs in it along with crumbled sausage, pepper Jack cheese, green onions, red bell pepper, and cayenne pepper.
2. Mix it all well.
3. Take two cake pans that fit inside the air fryer and grease it with oil spray.
4. Divide the omelet mixture between two cake pans.
5. Put the cake pans inside both of the Ninja Foodie 2-Basket Air Fryer baskets.
6. Turn on the BAKE function of the zone 1 basket and let it cook for 15-20 minutes at 310 degrees F.
7. Select MATCH button for zone 2 basket.
8. Once the cooking cycle is complete, take out, and serve hot as a delicious breakfast.
Serving Suggestion: Serve it with ketchup
Variation Tip: Use Parmesan cheese instead of Pepper Jack cheese
Nutritional Information Per Serving:
Calories 691| Fat 52.4g | Sodium 1122 mg | Carbs 13.3g | Fiber 1.8g| Sugar 7g | Protein 42g

Air Fried Sausage

Prep Time: 10 minutes.
Cook Time: 13 minutes.
Serves: 4
Ingredients:
• 4 sausage links, raw and uncooked
Preparation:
1. Divide the sausages in the two crisper plates.
2. Return the crisper plate to the Ninja Foodi Dual Zone Air Fryer.
3. Choose the Air Fry mode for Zone 1 and set the temperature to 390 degrees F and set the time to 13 minutes.
4. Select the "MATCH" button to copy the settings for Zone 2.
5. Initiate cooking by pressing the START/STOP button.
6. Serve warm and fresh.
Serving Suggestion: Serve the sausages with toasted bread and eggs.
Variation Tip: Add black pepper and salt for seasoning.
Nutritional Information Per Serving:
Calories 267 | Fat 12g |Sodium 165mg | Carbs 39g | Fiber 1.4g | Sugar 22g | Protein 3.3g

Sweet Potatoes Hash

Prep Time: 15 Minutes
Cook Time: 25 Minutes
Serves: 2
Ingredients:
• 450 grams sweet potatoes
• ½ white onion, diced
• 3 tablespoons olive oil
• 1 teaspoon smoked Paprika
• ¼ teaspoon cumin
• ⅓ teaspoon ground turmeric
• ¼ teaspoon garlic salt
• 1 cup guacamole
Preparation:
1. Peel and cut the potatoes into cubes.
2. Transfer the potatoes to a bowl and add oil, white onions, cumin, Paprika, turmeric, and garlic salt.
3. Put this mixture between both the baskets of the Ninja Foodie 2-Basket Air Fryer.
4. Set zone 1 to AIR FRY mode for 10 minutes at 390 degrees F.
5. Press the MATCH button for zone 2.
6. Take out the baskets and shake them well.
7. Set the timer to 15 minutes at 390 degrees F and AIR FRY again and MATCH for zone 2.
8. Once done, serve it with guacamole.
Serving Suggestion: Serve it with ketchup and omelet
Variation Tip: Use canola oil instead of olive oil
Nutritional Information Per Serving:
Calories 691 | Fat 49.7g| Sodium 596mg | Carbs 64g | Fiber15g | Sugar 19g | Protein 8.1g

Donuts

Prep Time: 5 minutes
Cook Time: 15 minutes
Serves: 6
Ingredients:
• 1 cup granulated sugar
• 2 tablespoons ground cinnamon
• 1 can refrigerated flaky buttermilk biscuits
• ¼ cup unsalted butter, melted
Preparation:
1. Combine the sugar and cinnamon in a small shallow bowl and set aside.
2. Remove the biscuits from the can and put them on a chopping board, separated. Cut holes in the center of each biscuit with a 1-inch round biscuit cutter (or a similarly sized bottle cap).
3. Place a crisper plate in each drawer. In each drawer, place 4 biscuits in a single layer. Insert the drawers into the unit.
4. Select zone 1, then AIR FRY, then set the temperature to 360°F with a 10-minute timer. To match zone 2 settings to zone 1, choose MATCH. To begin cooking, select START/STOP.
5. Remove the donuts from the drawers after the timer has finished.
Serving Suggestion: Serve the donuts with tea.
Variation Tip: You can add some ground nutmeg.
Nutritional Information Per Serving:
Calories 223 | Fat 8g | Sodium 150mg | Carbs 40g | Fiber 1.4g | Sugar 34.2g | Protein 0.8g

Breakfast Bacon

Prep Time: 10 minutes.
Cook Time: 14 minutes.
Serves: 4
Ingredients:
• ½ lb. bacon slices
Preparation:
1. Spread half of the bacon slices in each of the crisper plate evenly in a single layer.
2. Return the crisper plate to the Ninja Foodi Dual Zone Air Fryer.
3. Choose the Air Fry mode for Zone 1 and set the temperature to 390 degrees F and the time to 14 minutes.
4. Select the "MATCH" button to copy the settings for Zone 2.
5. Initiate cooking by pressing the START/STOP button.
6. Flip the crispy bacon once cooked halfway through, then resume cooking.
7. Serve.
Serving Suggestion: Serve the bacon with eggs and bread slices.
Variation Tip: Add salt and black pepper for seasoning.
Nutritional Information Per Serving:
Calories 273 | Fat 22g |Sodium 517mg | Carbs 3.3g | Fiber 0.2g | Sugar 1.4g | Protein 16.1g

Hash Browns

Prep Time: 5 minutes
Cook Time: 5 minutes
Serves: 4
Ingredients:
• 4 frozen hash browns patties
• Cooking oil spray of choice
Preparation:
1. Install a crisper plate in both drawers. Place half the hash browns in zone 1 and half in zone 2, then insert the drawers into the unit. Spray the hash browns with some cooking oil.
2. Select zone 1, select AIR FRY, set temperature to 390°F, and set time to 5 minutes.
3. Select MATCH to match zone 2 settings to zone 1. Press the START/STOP button to begin cooking.

4. When cooking is complete, remove the hash browns and serve.
Serving Suggestion: Serve with ketchup or any condiment of your choice.
Variation Tip: You can use coconut oil.
Nutritional Information Per Serving:
Calories 130 | Fat 7g | Sodium 300mg | Carbs 15g | Fiber 2g | Sugar 0g | Protein 1g

Breakfast Casserole

Prep Time: 5 Minutes
Cook Time: 10 Minutes
Serves: 4
Ingredients:
• 1 pound beef sausage, grounded
• ¼ cup diced white onion
• 1 diced green bell pepper
• 8 whole eggs, beaten
• ½ cup Colby Jack cheese, shredded
• ¼ teaspoon garlic salt
• Oil spray, for greasing
Preparation:
1. Take a bowl and add the grounded sausage to it.
2. Add in the diced onions, bell peppers, eggs and whisk it well.
3. Then season it with garlic salt.
4. Spray both the baskets of the air fryer with oil spray.
5. Divide this mixture among the baskets; remember to remove the crisper plates.
6. Top the mixture with cheese.
7. Now, turn ON the Ninja Foodie 2-Basket Air Fryer zone 1 and select AIR FRY mode and set the time to 10 minutes at 390 degrees F.
8. Select the MATCH button for zone 2 baskets, and hit START/STOP button.
9. Once the cooking cycle is complete, take out, and serve.
10. Serve and enjoy.
Serving Suggestion: Serve it with sour cream
Variation Tip: Use turkey sausages instead of beef sausages
Nutritional Information Per Serving:
Calories 699| Fat 59.1g | Sodium 1217 mg | Carbs 6.8g | Fiber 0.6g| Sugar 2.5g | Protein 33.1 g

Bacon and Eggs for Breakfast

Prep Time: 12 Minutes
Cook Time: 12 Minutes
Serves: 1

Ingredients:
• 4 strips of thick-sliced bacon
• 2 small eggs
• Salt and black pepper, to taste
• Oil spray for greasing ramekins

Preparation:
1. Take 2 ramekins and grease them with oil spray.
2. Crack eggs into a bowl and season with salt and black pepper.
3. Divide the egg mixture between the two ramekins.
4. Put the bacon slices into the Ninja Foodie 2-Basket Air Fryer zone 1 basket, and the ramekins in zone 2 basket.
5. Now for zone 1 set it to AIR FRY mode at 400 degrees F for 12 minutes.
6. For zone 2 set it to 350 degrees F for 8 minutes using AIR FRY mode.
7. Press the Syncbutton and press START/STOP button so they both finish at the same time.
8. Once done, serve and enjoy.

Serving Suggestion: None
Variation Tip: Use butter for greasing the ramekins
Nutritional Information Per Serving:
Calories 131 | Fat 10g| Sodium 187mg | Carbs 0.6 g | Fiber 0g | Sugar 0.6g | Protein 10.7

Air Fried Bacon and Eggs

Prep Time: 5 minutes
Cook Time: 10 minutes
Serves: 1

Ingredients:
• 2 eggs
• 2 slices bacon

Preparation:
1. Grease a ramekin using cooking spray.
2. Install the crisper plate in the zone 1 drawer and place the bacon inside it. Insert the drawer into the unit.
3. Crack the eggs and add them to the greased ramekin.
4. Install the crisper plate in the zone 2 drawer and place the ramekin inside it. Insert the drawer into the unit.
5. Select zone 1 to AIR FRY for 9–11 minutes at 400°F. Select zone 2 to AIR FRY for 8–9 minutes at 350°F. Press SYNC.
6. Press START/STOP to begin cooking.
7. Enjoy!

Serving Suggestion: Serve with slices of toast.
Variation Tip: You can use ham instead.
Nutritional Information Per Serving:
Calories 331 | Fat 24.5g | Sodium 1001mg | Carbs 1.2g | Fiber 0g | Sugar 0.7g | Protein 25.3g

Air Fryer Sausage Patties

Prep Time: 5 minutes
Cook Time: 10 minutes
Serves: 12

Ingredients:
• 1-pound pork sausage or ready-made patties
• Fennel seeds or preferred seasonings

Preparation:
1. Prepare the sausage by slicing it into patties, then flavor it with fennel seed or your favorite seasonings.
2. Install a crisper plate in both drawers. Place half the patties in zone 1 and half in zone 2, then insert the drawers into the unit.
3. Select zone 1, select AIR FRY, set temperature to 390°F, and set time to 10 minutes.
4. Select MATCH to match zone 2 settings to zone 1. Press the START/STOP button to begin cooking.
5. When cooking is complete, remove the patties from the unit and serve with sauce or make a burger.

Serving Suggestion: Serve in a burger bun.
Variation Tip: You can use chicken sausage instead.
Nutritional Information Per Serving:
Calories 130 | Fat 10.5g | Sodium 284mg | Carbs 0.3g | Fiber 0.2g | Sugar 0g | Protein 7.4g

Egg White Muffins

Prep Time: 15 minutes
Cook Time: 10 minutes
Serves: 8

Ingredients:
- 4 slices center-cut bacon, cut into strips
- 4 ounces baby bella mushrooms, roughly chopped
- 2 ounces sun-dried tomatoes
- 2 tablespoon sliced black olives
- 2 tablespoons grated or shredded parmesan
- 2 tablespoons shredded mozzarella
- ¼ teaspoon black pepper
- ¾ cup liquid egg whites
- 2 tablespoons liquid egg whites

Preparation:
1. Heat a saucepan with a little oil, add the bacon and mushrooms and cook until fully cooked and crispy, about 6–8 minutes.
2. While the bacon and mushrooms cook, mix the ¾ cup liquid egg whites, sun-dried tomato, olives, parmesan, mozzarella, and black pepper together in a large bowl.
3. Add the cooked bacon and mushrooms to the tomato and olive mixture, stirring everything together.
4. Spoon the mixture into muffin molds, followed by 2 tablespoons of egg whites over the top.
5. Place half the muffins mold in zone 1 and half in zone 2, then insert the drawers into the unit.
6. Select zone 1, select AIR FRY, set temperature to 390°F, and set time to 22 minutes.
7. Select MATCH to match zone 2 settings to zone 1. Press the START/STOP button to begin cooking.
8. When cooking is complete, remove the molds and enjoy!

Serving Suggestion: Serve the muffins with a sauce of your choice.

Variation Tip: You can also add shredded zucchini.

Nutritional Information Per Serving:
Calories 104 | Fat 5.6g | Sodium 269mg | Carbs 3.5g | Fiber 0.8g | Sugar 0.3g | Protein 10.3g

Egg with Baby Spinach

Prep Time: 12 Minutes
Cook Time: 12 Minutes
Serves: 4

Ingredients:
- Nonstick spray, for greasing ramekins
- 2 tablespoons olive oil
- 6 ounces baby spinach
- 2 garlic cloves, minced
- ⅓ teaspoon kosher salt
- 6-8 large eggs
- ½ cup half and half
- Salt and black pepper, to taste
- 8 Sourdough bread slices, toasted

Preparation:
1. Grease 4 ramekins with oil spray and set them aside for further use.
2. Take a skillet and heat oil in it.
3. Cook spinach for 2 minutes and add the garlic, salt and black pepper.
4. Let it simmer for 2 more minutes.
5. Once the spinach is wilted, transfer it to a plate.
6. Whisk the eggs in a small bowl.
7. Add in the spinach.
8. Whisk it well and then pour in the half and half.
9. Divide this mixture between 4 ramekins and remember not to overfill it to the top.
10. Put the ramekins in zone 1 and zone 2 baskets of the Ninja Foodie 2-Basket Air Fryer.
11. Press START/STOP button and set zone 1 to AIR FRY at 350 degrees F for 8-12 minutes.
12. Press the MATCH button for zone 2.
13. Once it's cooked and eggs are done, serve with sourdough bread slices.

Serving Suggestion: Serve it with cream cheese topping

Variation Tip: Use plain bread slices instead of sourdough bread slices

Nutritional Information Per Serving:
Calories 404| Fat 19.6g| Sodium 761mg | Carbs 40.1g | Fiber 2.5g| Sugar 2.5g | Protein 19.2g

Banana and Raisins Muffins

Prep Time: 20 Minutes
Cook Time: 16 Minutes
Serves: 2

Ingredients:
• Salt, pinch
• 2 eggs, whisked
• ⅓ cup butter, melted
• 4 tablespoons almond milk
• ¼ teaspoon vanilla extract
• ½ teaspoon baking powder
• 1-½ cup all-purpose flour
• 1 cup mashed bananas
• 2 tablespoons raisins

Preparation:
1. Take about 4 large (one-cup sized) ramekins and layer them with muffin papers.
2. Crack the eggs in a large bowl, and whisk it all well and addvanilla extract, almond milk, baking powder, and melted butter.
3. Whisk the Ingredients: in very well.
4. Take a separate bowl and add the all-purpose flour and salt.
5. Combine the dry Ingredients: with the wet Ingredients:.
6. Pour mashed bananas and raisins into the batter.
7. Mix it well to make a batter for the muffins.
8. Pour the batter into the four ramekins and divide the ramekins into the air fryer zones.
9. Set the timer for zone 1 to 16 minutes at 350 degrees F on AIR FRY mode.
10. Select the MATCH button for the zone 2 basket.
11. Check and if not done, and let it AIR FRY for one more minute.
12. Once it is done, serve.

Serving Suggestion: None
Variation Tip: None
Nutritional Information Per Serving:
Calories 727| Fat 43.1g| Sodium 366 mg | Carbs 74.4g | Fiber 4.7g | Sugar 16.1g | Protein 14.1g

Perfect Cinnamon Toast

Prep Time: 5 minutes
Cook Time: 10 minutes
Serves: 6

Ingredients:
• 12 slices whole-wheat bread
• 1 stick butter, room temperature
• ½ cup white sugar
• 1½ teaspoons ground cinnamon
• 1½ teaspoons pure vanilla extract
• 1 pinch kosher salt
• 2 pinches freshly ground black pepper (optional)

Preparation:
1. Mash the softened butter with a fork or the back of a spoon in a bowl. Add the sugar, cinnamon, vanilla, and salt. Stir until everything is well combined.
2. Spread one-sixth of the mixture onto each slice of bread, making sure to cover the entire surface.
3. Install a crisper plate in both drawers. Place half the bread sliced in the zone 1 drawer and half in the zone 2 drawer, then insert the drawers into the unit.
4. Select zone 1, select AIR FRY, set temperature to 400°F, and set time to 5 minutes. Select MATCH to match zone 2 settings to zone 1. Press the START/STOP button to begin cooking
5. When cooking is complete, remove the slices and cut them diagonally.
6. Serve immediately.

Serving Suggestion: Serve with maple syrup.
Variation Tip: You can use honey.
Nutritional Information Per Serving:
Calories 322 | Fat 16.5g | Sodium 249mg | Carbs 39.3g | Fiber 4.2g | Sugar 18.2g | Protein 8.2g

Pumpkin Muffins

Prep Time: 15 minutes.
Cook Time: 13 minutes.
Serves: 8

Ingredients:
- ½ cup pumpkin puree
- 1 cup gluten-free oats
- ¼ cup honey
- 1 medium egg beaten
- ½ teaspoon coconut butter
- ½ tablespoon cocoa nib
- ½ tablespoon vanilla essence
- Cooking spray
- ½ teaspoon nutmeg

Preparation:
1. Add oats, honey, eggs, pumpkin puree, coconut butter, cocoa nibs, vanilla essence, and nutmeg to a bowl and mix well until smooth.
2. Divide the batter into two 4-cup muffin trays, greased with cooking spray.
3. Place one mini muffin tray in each of the two crisper plates.
4. Return the crisper plates to the Ninja Foodi Dual Zone Air Fryer.
5. Choose the Air Fry mode for Zone 1 and set the temperature to 375 degrees F and the time to 13 minutes.
6. Select the "MATCH" button to copy the settings for Zone 2.
7. Initiate cooking by pressing the START/STOP button.
8. Allow the muffins to cool, then serve.

Serving Suggestion: Serve the muffins with a hot coffee.

Variation Tip: Add raisins and nuts to the batter before baking.

Nutritional Information Per Serving:
Calories 209 | Fat 7.5g |Sodium 321mg | Carbs 34.1g | Fiber 4g | Sugar 3.8g | Protein 4.3g

Egg and Avocado in The Ninja Foodi

Prep Time: 10 Minutes
Cook Time: 12 Minutes
Serves: 2

Ingredients:
- 2 avocados, pitted and cut in half
- Garlic salt, to taste
- Cooking oil for greasing
- 4 eggs
- ¼ teaspoon Paprika powder for sprinkling
- ⅓ cup Parmesan cheese, crumbled
- 6 bacon strips, raw

Preparation:
1. First, cut the avocado in half and pit it.
2. Now scoop out the flesh from the avocado and keep aside
3. Crack one egg in each hole of the avocado and sprinkle paprika and garlic salt.
4. Sprinkle it with cheese at the end.
5. Now put it into tin foils and then put it in the air fryer zone basket 1.
6. Put bacon strips in zone 2 basket.
7. Now for zone 1, set it to AIR FRY mode at 350 degrees F for 10 minutes.
8. Place the bacon in zone 2, set it to 400 degrees for 12 minutes on AIR FRY mode.
9. Press the Sync button and press START/STOP button so it will finish at the same time.
10. Once done, serve and enjoy.

Serving Suggestion: Serve it with bread slices

Variation Tip: Use butter for greasing

Nutritional Information Per Serving:
Calories 609 | Fat 53.2g | Sodium 335mg | Carbs 18.1g | Fiber 13.5g | Sugar 1.7g | Protein 21.3g

Cinnamon Toasts

Prep Time: 15 minutes.
Cook Time: 8 minutes.
Serves: 4
Ingredients:
• 4 pieces of bread
• 2 tablespoons butter
• 2 eggs, beaten
• 1 pinch salt
• 1 pinch cinnamon ground
• 1 pinch nutmeg ground
• 1 pinch ground clove
• 1 teaspoon icing sugar
Preparation:
1. Add two eggs to a mixing bowl and stir cinnamon, nutmeg, ground cloves, and salt, then whisk well.
2. Spread butter on both sides of the bread slices and cut them into thick strips.
3. Dip the breadsticks in the egg mixture and place them in the two crisper plates.
4. Return the crisper plates to the Ninja Foodi Dual Zone Air Fryer.
5. Choose the Air Fry mode for Zone 1 and set the temperature to 390 degrees F and the time to 8 minutes.
6. Select the "MATCH" button to copy the settings for Zone 2.
7. Initiate cooking by pressing the START/STOP button.
8. Flip the French toast sticks when cooked halfway through.
9. Serve.
Serving Suggestion: Serve the toasted with chocolate syrup or Nutella spread.
Variation Tip: Use crushed cornflakes for breading to have extra crispiness.
Nutritional Information Per Serving:
Calories 199 | Fat 11.1g |Sodium 297mg | Carbs 14.9g | Fiber 1g | Sugar 2.5g | Protein 9.9g

Bacon and Egg Omelet

Prep Time: 12 Minutes
Cook Time: 10 Minutes
Serves: 2
Ingredients:
• 2 eggs, whisked
• ½ teaspoon chopped tomatoes
• Sea salt and black pepper, to taste
• 2 teaspoons almond milk
• 1 teaspoon cilantro, chopped
• 1 small green chili, chopped
• 4 strips bacon
Preparation:
1. Take a bowl and whisk the eggs in it.
2. Then add the green chili, salt, black pepper, cilantro, almond milk, and chopped tomatoes.
3. Grease the ramekins with.
4. Pour this into ramekins.
5. Put the bacon in the zone 1 basket and ramekins in zone 2 basket of the Ninja Foodi2-Basket Air Fryer.
6. Now for zone 1, set it to AIR FRY mode at 400 degrees F for 10 minutes.
7. For zone 2, set it to 350 degrees for 10 minutes in AIR FRY mode.
8. Press theSync button and press START/STOP button so thatit will finish both at the same time.
9. Once done, serve and enjoy.
Serving Suggestion: Serve it with bread slices and ketchup
Variation Tip: Use garlic salt instead of sea salt
Nutritional Information Per Serving:
Calories 285| Fat 21.5g| Sodium 1000 mg | Carbs 2.2g | Fiber 0.1g| Sugar 1g | Protein 19.7g

Banana Muffins

Prep Time: 5 minutes
Cook Time: 15 minutes
Serves: 10

Ingredients:
- 2 very ripe bananas
- ⅓ cup olive oil
- 1 egg
- ½ cup brown sugar
- 1 teaspoon vanilla extract
- 1 teaspoon cinnamon
- ¾ cup self-rising flour

Preparation:
1. In a large mixing bowl, mash the bananas, then add the egg, brown sugar, olive oil, and vanilla. To blend, stir everything together thoroughly.
2. Fold in the flour and cinnamon until everything is just blended.
3. Fill muffin molds evenly with the mixture (silicone or paper).
4. Install a crisper plate in both drawers. Place the muffin molds in a single layer in each drawer. Insert the drawers into the unit.
5. Select zone 1, select AIR FRY, set temperature to 360°F, and set time to 15 minutes. Select MATCH to match zone 2 settings to zone 1. Select START/STOP to begin.
6. Once the timer has finished, remove the muffins from the drawers.
7. Serve and enjoy!

Serving Suggestion: Serve with a smoothie.
Variation Tip: You can use almond flour.
Nutritional Information Per Serving:
Calories 148 | Fat 7.3g | Sodium 9mg | Carbs 19.8g | Fiber 1g | Sugar 10g | Protein 1.8g

Bagels

Prep Time: 10 minutes
Cook Time: 15 minutes
Serves: 8

Ingredients:
- 2 cups self-rising flour
- 2 cups non-fat plain Greek yogurt
- 2 beaten eggs for egg wash (optional)
- ½ cup sesame seeds (optional)

Preparation:
1. In a medium mixing bowl, combine the self-rising flour and Greek yogurt using a wooden spoon.
2. Knead the dough for about 5 minutes on a lightly floured board.
3. Divide the dough into four equal pieces and roll each into a thin rope, securing the ends to form a bagel shape.
4. Install a crisper plate in both drawers. Place 4 bagels in a single layer in each drawer. Insert the drawers into the unit.
5. Select zone 1, select AIR FRY, set temperature to 360°F, and set time to 15 minutes. Select MATCH to match zone 2 settings to zone 1. Select START/STOP to begin.
6. Once the timer has finished, remove the bagels from the units.
7. Serve and enjoy!

Serving Suggestion: Serve with cream cheese.
Variation Tip: You can use all-purpose flour.
Nutritional Information Per Serving:
Calories 202 | Fat 4.5g | Sodium 55mg | Carbs 31.3g | Fiber 2.7g | Sugar 4.7g | Protein 8.7g

Chapter 2 Snack and Appetizer Recipes

Spicy Chicken Tenders

Prep Time: 15 Minutes
Cook Time: 12 Minutes
Serves: 2
Ingredients:
• 2 large eggs, whisked
• 2 tablespoons lemon juice
• Salt and black pepper
• 1 pound chicken tenders
• 1 cup Panko bread crumbs
• ½ cup Italian bread crumbs
• 1 teaspoon smoked Paprika
• ¼ teaspoon garlic powder
• ¼ teaspoon onion powder
• ½ cup fresh grated Parmesan cheese
Preparation:
1. Take a bowl and whisk the eggs and set aside.
2. In a large bowl, add lemon juice, Paprika, salt, black pepper, garlic powder, onion powder
3. In a separate bowl, mix Panko bread crumbs, Italian bread crumbs, and Parmesan cheese.
4. Dip the chicken tenders in the spice mixture and coat well.
5. Let the tenders sit for 1 hour.
6. Dip each tender into the egg mixture and then into the bread crumbs.
7. Line both the baskets of the air fryer with parchment paper.
8. Divide the tenders between the baskets.
9. Set zone 1 basket to AIR FRY mode at 350 degrees F for 12 minutes.
10. Select the MATCH button for the zone 2 basket.
11. Once it's done, serve.
Serving Suggestion: Serve it with ketchup
Variation Tip: Use mild Paprika instead of smoked Paprika
Nutritional Information Per Serving:
Calories 836| Fat 36g| Sodium 1307 mg | Carbs 31.3g | Fiber 2.5g| Sugar 3.3 g | Protein 95.3g

Mozzarella Sticks

Prep Time: 1 hour 10 minutes
Cook Time: 1 hour 15 minutes
Serves: 8
Ingredients:
• 8 mozzarella sticks
• ¼ cup all-purpose flour
• 1 egg, whisked
• 1 cup panko breadcrumbs
• ½ teaspoon each onion powder, garlic powder, smoked paprika, salt
Preparation:
1. Freeze the mozzarella sticks for 30 minutes after placing them on a parchment-lined plate.
2. In the meantime, set up your "breading station": Fill a Ziploc bag halfway with flour. In a small dish, whisk the egg. In a separate shallow bowl, combine the panko and spices.
3. To bread your mozzarella sticks: Toss the sticks into the bag of flour, seal it, and shake to coat the cheese evenly. Take out the sticks and dip them in the egg, then in the panko, one at a time. Put the coated sticks back on the plate and put them in the freezer for another 30 minutes.
4. Place a crisper plate in each drawer, then add the mozzarella sticks in a single layer to each. Insert the drawers into the unit.
5. Select zone 1, then AIR FRY, then set the temperature to 400°F with a 15-minute timer. To match zone 2 settings to zone 1, choose MATCH. To begin, select START/STOP
Serving Suggestion: Serve with a sauce of your choice.
Variation Tip: You can use coconut flour if you prefer.
Nutritional Information Per Serving:
Calories 131 | Fat 5.3g | Sodium 243mg | Carbs 11.3g | Fiber 1.1g | Sugar 0.3g | Protein 9.9g

Dijon Cheese Sandwich

Prep Time: 10 Minutes
Cook Time: 10 Minutes
Serves: 2

Ingredients:
• 4 large slices sourdough, whole grain
• 4 tablespoons Dijon mustard
• 1-½ cup grated sharp Cheddar cheese
• 2 teaspoons green onion, green part chopped off
• 2 tablespoons butter melted

Preparation:
1. Brush the melted butter on one side of all the bread slices.
2. Spread Dijon mustard on the other side of the slices.
3. Top the 2 bread slices with Cheddar cheese and top it with green onions.
4. Cover with the remaining two slices to make two sandwiches.
5. Place one sandwich in each basket of the air fryer.
6. Turn to AIR FRY mode for zone 1 basket at 350 degrees F for 10 minutes.
7. Use the MATCH button for zone 2.
8. Once it's done, serve.

Serving Suggestion: Serve with tomato soup
Variation Tip: Use oil spray instead of butter
Nutritional Information Per Serving:
Calories 617| Fat 38g| Sodium 1213mg | Carbs 40.8g | Fiber 5g| Sugar 5.6g | Protein 29.5g

Stuffed Bell Peppers

Prep Time: 25 Minutes
Cook Time: 16 Minutes
Serves: 3

Ingredients:
• 6 large bell peppers
• 1-½ cups cooked rice
• 2 cups Cheddar cheese

Preparation:
1. Cut the bell peppers in half lengthwise and remove all the seeds.
2. Fill the cavity of each bell pepper with cooked rice.
3. Divide the bell peppers into the two zones of the air fryer baskets.

4. Set the time for zone 1 for 200 degrees F for 10 minutes on AIR FRY mode.
5. Select MATCH button of zone 2 basket.
6. Take out the baskets and sprinkle cheese on top.
7. Set the time for zone 1 for 200 degrees for 6 more minutes on AIR FRY.
8. Select MATCH button of zone 2 basket.
9. Once it's done, serve.

Serving Suggestion: Serve it mashed potatoes
Variation Tip: You can use any cheese you like
Nutritional Information Per Serving:
Calories 605| Fat 26g | Sodium 477mg | Carbs 68.3g | Fiber 4g| Sugar 12.5g | Protein 25.6 g

Sweet Bites

Prep Time: 25 Minutes
Cook Time: 12 Minutes
Serves: 4

Ingredients:
• 10 sheets Phyllo dough, (filo dough)
• 2 tablespoons melted butter
• 1 cup walnuts, chopped
• 2 teaspoons honey
• 1 Pinch of cinnamon
• 1 teaspoon orange zest

Preparation:
1. First, layer together 10 Phyllo dough sheets on a flat surface.
2. Then cut it into 4 *4-inch squares.
3. Coat the squares with butter then drizzle some honey, orange zest, walnuts, and cinnamon on top.
4. Bring all 4 corners together and press the corners to make a little purse like design.
5. Divide them into both the air fryer baskets and select zone 1 to AIR FRY mode, and set it for 7 minutes at 375 degrees F.
6. Select the MATCH button for the zone 2 basket.
7. Once done, take out and serve.

Serving Suggestion: Serve with a topping of nuts
Variation Tip: None
Nutritional Information Per Serving:
Calories 397| Fat 27.1 g| Sodium 271mg | Carbs 31.2 g | Fiber 3.2g| Sugar 3.3g | Protein 11g

Cheddar Quiche

Prep Time: 10 Minutes
Cook Time: 12 Minutes
Serves: 2
Ingredients:
• 4 eggs, organic
• 1-¼ cup heavy cream
• Salt, pinch
• ½ cup broccoli florets
• ½ cup Cheddar cheese, shredded and for sprinkling
Preparation:
1. Take a Pyrex pitcher and crack two eggs into it.
2. Fill it with heavy cream, about half the way up.
3. Add in the salt and then the broccoli.
4. Pour the mixture into two quiche dishes, and top it with shredded Cheddar cheese.
5. Divide it into both zones of the baskets.
6. For zone 1, set the time to 10-12 minutes at 325 degrees F on AIR FRY mode.
7. Select the MATCH button for the zone 2 basket.
8. Once done, serve hot.
Serving Suggestion: Serve with herbs as a topping
Variation Tip: Use spinach instead of broccoli florets
Nutritional Information Per Serving:
Calories 454| Fat 40g | Sodium 406mg | Carbs 4.2g | Fiber 0.6g| Sugar 1.3 g | Protein 20g

Ravioli

Prep Time: 5 minutes
Cook Time: 6 minutes
Serves: 2
Ingredients:
• 12 frozen portions of ravioli
• ½ cup buttermilk
• ½ cup Italian breadcrumbs
Preparation:
1. Place two bowls side by side. Put the buttermilk in one and breadcrumbs in the other.
2. Dip each piece of ravioli into the buttermilk then breadcrumbs, making sure to coat them as best as possible.

3. Place a crisper plate in both drawers. In each drawer, put four breaded ravioli pieces in a single layer. Insert the drawers into the unit.
4. Select zone 1, then AIR FRY, then set the temperature to 360°F with a 6-minute timer. To match zone 2 settings to zone 1, choose MATCH. To begin, select START/STOP.
5. Remove the ravioli from the drawers after the timer has finished.
Serving Suggestion: Serve with your favorite pasta sauce.
Variation Tip: You can use panko breadcrumbs.
Nutritional Information Per Serving:
Calories 481 | Fat 20g | Sodium 1162mg | Carbs 56g | Fiber 4g | Sugar 9g | Protein 19g

Fried Pickles

Prep Time: 10 minutes
Cook Time: 15 minutes
Serves: 4
Ingredients:
• 2 cups sliced dill pickles
• 1 cup flour
• 1 tablespoon garlic powder
• 1 tablespoon Cajun spice
• ½ tablespoon cayenne pepper
• Olive Oil or cooking spray
Preparation:
1. Mix together the flour and spices in a bowl.
2. Coat the sliced pickles with the flour mixture.
3. Place a crisper plate in each drawer. Put the pickles in a single layer in each drawer. Insert the drawers into the unit.
4. Select zone 1, then AIR FRY, then set the temperature to 400°F with a 15-minute timer. To match zone 2 settings to zone 1, choose MATCH. To begin, select START/STOP.
Serving Suggestion: Serve with a dipping sauce of your choice.
Variation Tip: You can use coconut flour.
Nutritional Information Per Serving:
Calories 161 | Fat 4.1g | Sodium 975mg | Carbs 27.5g | Fiber 2.2g | Sugar 1.5g | Protein 4g

Mac and Cheese Balls

Prep Time: 15 minutes
Cook Time: 20 minutes
Serves: 4

Ingredients:
- 1 cup panko breadcrumbs
- 4 cups prepared macaroni and cheese, refrigerated
- 3 tablespoons flour
- 1 teaspoon salt, divided
- 1 teaspoon ground black pepper, divided
- 1 teaspoon smoked paprika, divided
- ½ teaspoon garlic powder, divided
- 2 eggs
- 1 tablespoon milk
- ¼ cup ranch dressing, garlic aioli, or chipotle mayo, for dipping (optional)

Preparation:
1. Preheat a conventional oven to 400°F.
2. Shake the breadcrumbs onto a baking sheet so that they're evenly distributed. Bake in the oven for 3 minutes, then shake and bake for an additional 1 to 2 minutes, or until toasted.
3. Form the chilled macaroni and cheese into golf ball-sized balls and set them aside.
4. Combine the flour, ½ teaspoon salt, ½ teaspoon black pepper, ½ teaspoon smoked paprika, and ¼ teaspoon garlic powder in a large mixing bowl.
5. In a small bowl, whisk together the eggs and milk.
6. Combine the breadcrumbs, remaining salt, pepper, paprika, and garlic powder in a mixing bowl.
7. To coat the macaroni and cheese balls, roll them in the flour mixture, then the egg mixture, and then the breadcrumb mixture.
8. Place a crisper plate in each drawer. Put the cheese balls in a single layer in each drawer. Insert the drawers into the unit.
9. Select zone 1, then AIR FRY, then set the temperature to 360°F with an 8-minute timer. To match zone 2 settings to zone 1, choose MATCH. To begin, select START/STOP.
10. Serve and enjoy!

Serving Suggestion: Serve with a dipping sauce of your choice.
Variation Tip: You can use whole-wheat or Italian seasoned breadcrumbs.
Nutritional Information Per Serving:
Calories 489 | Fat 15.9g | Sodium 1402mg | Carbs 69.7g | Fiber 2.5g | Sugar 4g | Protein 16.9g

Cauliflower Gnocchi

Prep Time: 15 minutes.
Cook Time: 17 minutes.
Serves: 5

Ingredients:
- 1 bag frozen cauliflower gnocchi
- 1 ½ tablespoons olive oil
- 1 teaspoon garlic powder
- 3 tablespoons parmesan, grated
- ½ teaspoon dried basil
- Salt to taste
- Fresh chopped parsley for topping

Preparation:
1. Toss gnocchi with olive oil, garlic powder, 1 tablespoon of parmesan, salt, and basil in a bowl.
2. Divide the gnocchi in the two crisper plate.
3. Return the crisper plate to the Ninja Foodi Dual Zone Air Fryer.
4. Choose the Air Fry mode for Zone 1 and set the temperature to 400 degrees F and the time to 10 minutes.
5. Select the "MATCH" button to copy the settings for Zone 2.
6. Initiate cooking by pressing the START/STOP button.
7. Toss the gnocchi once cooked halfway through, then resume cooking.
8. Drizzle the remaining parmesan on top of the gnocchi and cook again for 7 minutes.
9. Serve warm.

Serving Suggestion: Serve with tomato or sweet chili sauce.
Variation Tip: Use crushed cornflakes for breading to have extra crispiness.
Nutritional Information Per Serving:
Calories 134 | Fat 5.9g |Sodium 343mg | Carbs 9.5g | Fiber 0.5g | Sugar 1.1g | Protein 10.4g

Chicken Tenders

Prep Time: 15 Minutes
Cook Time: 12 Minutes
Serves: 3
Ingredients:
• 1 pound chicken tenders
• Salt and black pepper, to taste
• 1 cup Panko bread crumbs
• 2 cups Italian bread crumbs
• 1 cup Parmesan cheese
• 2 eggs
• Oil spray, for greasing
Preparation:
1. Sprinkle the tenders with salt and black pepper.
2. In a medium bowl mix the Panko bread crumbs with Italian bread crumbs.
3. Add salt, pepper, and Parmesan cheese.
4. Crack two eggs into a bowl.
5. Dip the chicken tenders into the eggs and then into the bread crumbs and spray with oil spray.
6. Line both of the baskets of the air fryer with parchment paper.
7. Divide the tenders between the baskets of Ninja Foodi 2-Basket Air Fryer.
8. Set zone 1 basket to AIR FRY mode at 350 degrees F for 12 minutes.
9. Select the MATCH button for the zone 2 basket.
10. Once it's done, serve.
Serving Suggestion: Serve it with ranch or ketchup
Variation Tip: Use Italian seasoning instead of Italian bread crumbs
Nutritional Information Per Serving:
Calories 558 | Fat 23.8g | Sodium 872mg | Carbs 20.9g | Fiber 1.7 g| Sugar 2.2 g | Protein 63.5g

Grill Cheese Sandwich

Prep Time: 15 Minutes
Cook Time: 10 Minutes
Serves: 2
Ingredients:
• 4 white bread slices
• 2 tablespoons butter, melted
• 2 slices sharp Cheddar
• 2 slices Swiss cheese
• 2 slices Mozzarella cheese

Preparation:
1. Brush melted butter on one side of all the bread slices and then top the 2 bread slices with Cheddar, Swiss, and mozzarella.
2. Top it with the other slice to make a sandwich.
3. Divide it between the two baskets of the air fryer.
4. Turn toAIR FRY mode for zone 1 basket at 350 degrees F for 10 minutes.
5. Use the MATCH button for zone 2.
6. Once done, serve.
Serving Suggestion: Serve with tomato soup
Variation Tip: Use oil spray instead of butter
Nutritional Information Per Serving:
Calories 577 | Fat 38g | Sodium 1466mg | Carbs 30.5g | Fiber 1.1g| Sugar 6.5g | Protein 27.6g

Fried Halloumi Cheese

Prep Time: 10 minutes.
Cook Time: 12 minutes.
Serves: 6
Ingredients:
• 1 block of halloumi cheese, sliced
• 2 teaspoons olive oil
Preparation:
1. Divide the halloumi cheese slices in the crisper plate.
2. Drizzle olive oil over the cheese slices.
3. Return the crisper plate to the Ninja Foodi Dual Zone Air Fryer.
4. Choose the Air Fry mode for Zone 1 and set the temperature to 360 degrees F and the time to 12 minutes.
5. Flip the cheese slices once cooked halfway through.
6. Serve.
Serving Suggestion: Serve with fresh yogurt dip or cucumber salad.
Variation Tip: Add black pepper and salt for seasoning.
Nutritional Information Per Serving:
Calories 186 | Fat 3g |Sodium 223mg | Carbs 31g | Fiber 8.7g | Sugar 5.5g | Protein 9.7g

Parmesan Crush Chicken

Prep Time: 20 Minutes
Cook Time: 18 Minutes
Serves: 4
Ingredients:
• 4 chicken breasts
• 1 cup Parmesan cheese
• 1 cup bread crumbs
• 2 eggs, whisked
• Salt, to taste
• Oil spray, for greasing
Preparation:
1. Whisk the eggs in a large bowl and set aside.
2. Season the chicken breasts with salt and then dip them in the egg wash.
3. Next, dredge them with the breadcrumbs then Parmesan cheese.
4. Line both the baskets of the air fryer with parchment paper.
5. Divide the breasts between the baskets, and oil spray the breast pieces.
6. Set zone 1 basket to AIR FRY mode at 350 degrees F for 18 minutes.
7. Select the MATCH button for the zone 2 basket.
8. Once it's done, serve.
Serving Suggestion: Serve them with ketchup
Variation Tip: Use Cheddar cheese instead of Parmesan
Nutritional Information Per Serving:
Calories 574 | Fat 25g | Sodium 848mg | Carbs 21.4g | Fiber 1.2g| Sugar 1.8g | Protein 64.4g

Tater Tots

Prep Time: 10 minutes
Cook Time: 8 minutes
Serves: 4
Ingredients:
• 16 ounces tater tots
• ½ cup shredded cheddar cheese
• 1½ teaspoons bacon bits
• 2 green onions, chopped
• Sour cream (optional)
Preparation:
1. Place a crisper plate in each drawer. Put the tater tots into the drawers in a single layer. Insert the drawers into the unit.
2. Select zone 1, then AIR FRY, then set the temperature to 360°F with a 6-minute timer. To match zone 2 settings to zone 1, choose MATCH. To begin, select START/STOP.
3. When the cooking time is over, add the shredded cheddar cheese, bacon bits, and green onions over the tater tots. Select zone 1, AIR FRY, 360°F, for 4 minutes. Select MATCH. Press START/STOP.
4. Drizzle sour cream over the top before serving.
5. Enjoy!
Serving Suggestion: Serve sprinkled with some chopped parsley.
Variation Tip: You can use scallions.
Nutritional Information Per Serving:
Calories 335 | Fat 19.1g | Sodium 761mg | Carbs 34.1g | Fiber 3g | Sugar 0.6g | Protein 8.9g

Peppered Asparagus

Prep Time: 10 minutes.
Cook Time: 16 minutes.
Serves: 6
Ingredients:
• 1 bunch of asparagus, trimmed
• Avocado or Olive Oil
• Himalayan salt, to taste
• Black pepper, to taste
Preparation:
1. Divide the asparagus in the two crisper plate.
2. Toss the asparagus with salt, black pepper, and oil.
3. Return the crisper plate to the Ninja Foodi Dual Zone Air Fryer.
4. Choose the Air Fry mode for Zone 1 and set the temperature to 390 degrees F and the time to 16 minutes.
5. Select the "MATCH" button to copy the settings for Zone 2.
6. Initiate cooking by pressing the START/STOP button.
7. Serve warm.
Serving Suggestion: Serve with mayonnaise or cream cheese dip.
Variation Tip: Use panko crumbs for breading to have extra crispiness.
Nutritional Information Per Serving:
Calories 163 | Fat 11.5g |Sodium 918mg | Carbs 8.3g | Fiber 4.2g | Sugar 0.2g | Protein 7.4g

Jalapeño Popper Chicken

Prep Time: 20 minutes
Cook Time: 50 minutes
Serves: 4
Ingredients:
• 2 ounces cream cheese, softened
• ¼ cup shredded cheddar cheese
• ¼ cup shredded mozzarella cheese
• ¼ teaspoon garlic powder
• 4 small jalapeño peppers, seeds removed and diced
• Kosher salt, as desired
• Ground black pepper, as desired
• 4 organic boneless, skinless chicken breasts
• 8 slices bacon
Preparation:
1. Cream together the cream cheese, cheddar cheese, mozzarella cheese, garlic powder, and jalapeño in a mixing bowl. Add salt and pepper to taste.
2. Make a deep pocket in the center of each chicken breast, but be cautious not to cut all the way through.
3. Fill each chicken breast's pocket with the cream cheese mixture.
4. Wrap two strips of bacon around each chicken breast and attach them with toothpicks.
5. Place a crisper plate in each drawer. Put the chicken breasts in the drawers. Place both drawers in the unit.
6. Select zone 1, then AIR FRY, and set the temperature to 350°F with a 30-minute timer. To match zone 2 and zone 1 settings, select MATCH. To begin cooking, press the START/STOP button.
7. When cooking is complete, remove the chicken breasts and allow them to rest for 5 minutes before serving
Serving Suggestion: Serve with a dipping sauce of your choice.
Variation Tip: You can use turkey breasts instead.
Nutritional Information Per Serving:
Calories 507 | Fat 27.5g | Sodium 1432mg | Carbs 2.3g | Fiber 0.6g | Sugar 0.6g | Protein 58.2g

Stuffed Mushrooms

Prep Time: 7 minutes
Cook Time: 8 minutes
Serves: 5
Ingredients:
• 8 ounces fresh mushrooms (I used Monterey)
• 4 ounces cream cheese
• ¼ cup shredded parmesan cheese
• $^1/_8$ cup shredded sharp cheddar cheese
• $^1/_8$ cup shredded white cheddar cheese
• 1 teaspoon Worcestershire sauce
• 2 garlic cloves, minced
• Salt and pepper, to taste
Preparation:
1. To prepare the mushrooms for stuffing, remove their stems. Make a circle cut around the area where the stem used to be. Continue to cut until all of the superfluous mushroom is removed.
2. To soften the cream cheese, microwave it for 15 seconds.
3. Combine the cream cheese, shredded cheeses, salt, pepper, garlic, and Worcestershire sauce in a medium mixing bowl. To blend, stir everything together.
4. Stuff the mushrooms with the cheese mixture.
5. Place a crisper plate in each drawer. Put the stuffed mushrooms in a single layer in each drawer. Insert the drawers into the unit.
6. Select zone 1, then AIR FRY, then set the temperature to 360°F with an 8-minute timer. To match zone 2 settings to zone 1, choose MATCH. To begin, select START/STOP.
7. Serve and enjoy!
Serving Suggestion: Serve with a green salad.
Variation Tip: You can use soy sauce instead of Worcestershire.
Nutritional Information Per Serving:
Calories 230 | Fat 9.5g | Sodium 105mg | Carbs 35.5g | Fiber 5.1g | Sugar 0.1g | Protein 7.1g

Strawberries and Walnuts Muffins

Prep Time: 15 Minutes
Cook Time: 15 Minutes
Serves: 2
Ingredients:
• Salt, pinch
• 2 eggs, whisked
• ⅓ cup maple syrup
• ⅓ cup coconut oil
• 4 tablespoons water
• 1 teaspoon orange zest
• ¼ teaspoon vanilla extract
• ½ teaspoon baking powder
• 1 cup all-purpose flour
• 1 cup strawberries, finely chopped
• ⅓ cup walnuts, chopped and roasted
Preparation:
1. Layer 4 ramekins with muffin paper.
2. Add egg, maple syrup, oil, water, vanilla extract, and orange zest to a bowl and mix well.
3. In a separate bowl, mix flour, baking powder, and salt.
4. Add the dry Ingredients: slowly to the wet Ingredients:.
5. Pour the batter into the ramekins and top with strawberries and walnuts.
6. Divide the ramekins into both zones. For zone 1, set to AIR FRY mode at 350 degrees F for 15 minutes.
7. Select the MATCH button for the zone 2 basket.
8. Check and if not done, let it AIR FRY for one more minute.
9. Once done, serve.
Serving Suggestion: Serve it with coffee
Variation Tip: Use vegetable oil instead of coconut oil
Nutritional Information Per Serving:
Calories 897| Fat 53.9g | Sodium 148mg | Carbs 92g | Fiber 4.7g| Sugar 35.6 g | Protein 17.5g

Blueberries Muffins

Prep Time: 15 Minutes
Cook Time: 15 Minutes
Serves: 2
Ingredients:
• Salt, 1 pinch
• 2 eggs
• ⅓ cup sugar
• ⅓ cup vegetable oil
• 4 tablespoons water
• 1 teaspoon lemon zest
• ¼ teaspoon vanilla extract
• ½ teaspoon baking powder
• 1 cup all-purpose flour
• 1 cup blueberries
Preparation:
1. Take 4 ramekins that are oven safe and layer them with muffin papers.
2. Take a bowl and whisk the egg, sugar, oil, water, vanilla extract, and lemon zest in.
3. Whisk it all very well.
4. In a separate bowl, mix the flour, baking powder, and salt.
5. Add the dry Ingredients: slowly to the wet Ingredients:.
6. Pour the batter into the ramekins and top with blueberries.
7. Divide them between both zones of the Ninja Foodi 2-Basket Air Fryer.
8. Set the time for zone 1 to 15 minutes at 350 degrees F on AIR FRY mode.
9. Select the MATCH button for the zone 2 basket.
10. Check if not done, and let it AIR FRY for one more minute.
11. Once it is done, serve.
Serving Suggestion: Serve it with whipped cream topping
Variation Tip: Use butter instead of vegetable oil
Nutritional Information Per Serving:
Calories 781| Fat 41.6g | Sodium 143mg | Carbs 92.7g | Fiber 3.5g| Sugar41.2 g | Protein 0g

Garlic Bread

Prep Time: 7 minutes
Cook Time: 10 minutes
Serves: 4

Ingredients:
- ½ loaf of bread
- 3 tablespoons butter, softened
- 3 garlic cloves, minced
- ½ teaspoon Italian seasoning
- Small pinch of red pepper flakes

Optional
- ¼ cup shredded mozzarella cheese
- Freshly grated parmesan cheese
- Chopped fresh parsley for serving/topping

Preparation:
1. Slice the bread in half horizontally or as appropriate to fit inside the air fryer.
2. Combine the softened butter, garlic, Italian seasoning, and red pepper flakes in a mixing bowl.
3. Brush the garlic butter mixture evenly over the bread.
4. Place a crisper plate in each drawer. Place the bread pieces into each drawer. Insert the drawers into the unit.
5. Select zone 1, then AIR FRY, then set the temperature to 360°F with a 6-minute timer. To match zone 2 settings to zone 1, choose MATCH. To begin, select START/STOP.
6. Remove the garlic bread from your air fryer, slice, and serve!

Serving Suggestion: Serve with a sauce of your choice.

Variation Tip: You can use garlic salt for seasoning.

Nutritional Information Per Serving:
Calories 150 | Fat 8.2g | Sodium 208mg | Carbs 14.3g | Fiber 2.3g | Sugar 1.2g | Protein 4.9g

Crispy Chickpeas

Prep Time: 10 minutes
Cook Time: 15 minutes
Serves: 4

Ingredients:
- 1 (15-ounce) can unsalted chickpeas, rinsed and drained
- 1½ tablespoons toasted sesame oil
- ¼ teaspoon smoked paprika
- ¼ teaspoon crushed red pepper
- ⅛ teaspoon salt
- Cooking spray
- 2 lime wedges

Preparation:
1. The chickpeas should be spread out over multiple layers of paper towels. Roll the chickpeas under the paper towels to dry both sides, then top with more paper towels and pat until completely dry.
2. In a medium mixing bowl, combine the chickpeas and oil. Add the paprika, crushed red pepper, and salt to taste.
3. Place a crisper plate in each drawer. Put the chickpeas in a single layer in each drawer. Insert the drawers into the unit.
4. Select zone 1, then ROAST, then set the temperature to 400°F with a 15-minute timer. To match zone 2 settings to zone 1, choose MATCH. To begin, select START/STOP.

Serving Suggestion: Serve with roasted veggies.

Variation Tip: You can use garlic powder.

Nutritional Information Per Serving:
Calories 169 | Fat 5g | Sodium 357mg | Carbs 27.3g | Fiber 5.7g | Sugar 0.6g | Protein 5.9g

Zucchini Chips

Prep Time: 10 minutes
Cook Time: 15 minutes
Serves: 4

Ingredients:
- 1 medium-sized zucchini
- ½ cup panko breadcrumbs
- ½ teaspoon garlic powder
- ¼ teaspoon onion powder
- 1 egg
- 3 tablespoons flour

Preparation:
1. Slice the zucchini into thin slices, about ¼-inch thick.
2. In a mixing bowl, combine the panko breadcrumbs, garlic powder, and onion powder.
3. The egg should be whisked in a different bowl, while the flour should be placed in a third bowl.
4. Dip the zucchini slices in the flour, then in the egg, and finally in the breadcrumbs.
5. Place a crisper plate in each drawer. Put the zucchini slices into each drawer in a single layer. Insert the drawers into the unit.
6. Select zone 1, then AIR FRY, then set the temperature to 360°F with a 6-minute timer. To match zone 2 settings to zone 1, choose MATCH. To begin, select START/STOP.
7. Remove the zucchini from the drawers after the timer has finished.

Serving Suggestion: Serve the chips with mayo.

Variation Tip: You can use coconut flour if you prefer.

Nutritional Information Per Serving:
Calories 82 | Fat 1.5g | Sodium 89mg | Carbs 14.1g | Fiber 1.7g | Sugar 1.2g | Protein 3.9g

Chapter 3 Vegetable and Sides Recipes

Fresh Mix Veggies in Air Fryer

Prep Time: 15Minutes
Cook Time: 12 Minutes
Serves: 4
Ingredients: :
• 1 cup cauliflower florets
• 1 cup carrots, peeled chopped
• 1 cup broccoli florets
• 2 tablespoons avocado oil
• Salt, to taste
• ½ teaspoon chili powder
• ½ teaspoon garlic powder
• ½ teaspoon herbs de Provence
• 1 cup Parmesan cheese
Preparation:
1. Take a bowl, and add all the veggies to it.
2. Toss and then season the veggies with salt, chili powder, garlic powder, and herbs de Provence.
3. Toss it all well and then drizzle avocado oil.
4. Make sure the Ingredients: are coated well.
5. Distribute the veggies among both baskets of the air fryer.
6. Turn on the START/STOP button and set it to AIR FRY mode at 390 degrees F for 10-12 minutes.
7. For the zone 2 basket setting, press the MATCH button.
8. After 8 minutes of cooking, press the START/STOP button and then take out the baskets and sprinkle Parmesan cheese on top of the veggies.
9. Then let the cooking cycle complete for the next 3-4 minutes.
10. Once done, serve.
Serving Suggestion: Serve the veggies with rice
Variation Tip: Use canola oil or butter instead of avocado oil
Nutritional Information Per Serving:
Calories 161 | Fat 9.3g| Sodium 434mg | Carbs 7.7g | Fiber 2.4g | Sugar 2.5g | Protein 13.9

Zucchini with Stuffing

Prep Time: 12 Minutes
Cook Time: 20 Minutes
Serves: 3
Ingredients:
• 1 cup quinoa, rinsed
• 1 cup black olives
• 6 medium zucchinis, about 2 pounds
• 2 cups cannellini beans, drained
• 1 white onion, chopped
• ¼ cup almonds, chopped
• 4 cloves garlic, chopped
• 4 tablespoons olive oil
• 1 cup water
• 2 cups Parmesan cheese, for topping
Preparation:
1. First wash the zucchini and cut it lengthwise.
2. Take a skillet and heat oil in it.
3. Sauté the onion in olive oil for a few minutes.
4. Then add the quinoa and water and let it cook for 8 minutes with the lid on top.
5. Transfer the quinoa to a bowl and add all the remaining Ingredients:, excluding zucchini and Parmesan cheese.
6. Scoop out the seeds of the zucchinis.
7. Fill the cavity of zucchinis with the quinoa mixture.
8. Top it with a handful of Parmesan cheese.
9. Arrange the zucchinis in both air fryer baskets.
10. Select zone 1 basket at AIR FRY mode for 20 minutes and temperature to 390 degrees F.
11. Use the MATCH button to select the same setting for zone 2.
12. Serve and enjoy.
Serving Suggestion: Serve them with pasta
Variation Tip: None
Nutritional Information Per Serving:
Calories 1171| Fat 48.6g| Sodium 1747mg | Carbs 132.4g | Fiber 42.1g | Sugar 11.5g | Protein 65.7g

Quinoa Patties

Prep Time: 15 minutes.
Cook Time: 32 minutes.
Serves: 4
Ingredients:
- 1 cup quinoa red
- 1½ cups water
- 1 teaspoon salt
- black pepper, ground
- 1½ cups rolled oats
- 3 eggs beaten
- ¼ cup minced white onion
- ½ cup crumbled feta cheese
- ¼ cup chopped fresh chives
- Salt and black pepper, to taste
- Vegetable or canola oil
- 4 hamburger buns
- 4 arugulas
- 4 slices tomato sliced

Cucumber yogurt dill sauce
- 1 cup cucumber, diced
- 1 cup Greek yogurt
- 2 teaspoons lemon juice
- ¼ teaspoon salt
- Black pepper, ground
- 1 tablespoon chopped fresh dill
- 1 tablespoon olive oil

Preparation:
1. Add quinoa to a saucepan filled with cold water, salt, and black pepper, and place it over medium-high heat.
2. Cook the quinoa to a boil, then reduce the heat, cover, and cook for 20 minutes on a simmer.
3. Fluff and mix the cooked quinoa with a fork and remove it from the heat.
4. Spread the quinoa in a baking stay.
5. Mix eggs, oats, onion, herbs, cheese, salt, and black pepper.
6. Stir in quinoa, then mix well. Make 4 patties out of this quinoa cheese mixture.
7. Divide the patties in the two crisper plates and spray them with cooking oil.
8. Return the crisper plates to the Ninja Foodi Dual Zone Air Fryer.
9. Choose the Air Fry mode for Zone 1 and set the temperature to 390 degrees F and the time to 13 minutes.
10. Select the "MATCH" button to copy the settings for Zone 2.
11. Initiate cooking by pressing the START/STOP button.
12. Flip the patties once cooked halfway through, and resume cooking.
13. Meanwhile, prepare the cucumber yogurt dill sauce by mixing all of its Ingredients: in a mixing bowl.
14. Place each quinoa patty in a burger bun along with arugula leaves.
15. Serve with yogurt dill sauce.
Serving Suggestion: Serve with yogurt dip.
Variation Tip: Use crushed cornflakes for breading to have extra crispiness.
Nutritional Information Per Serving:
Calories 231 | Fat 9g |Sodium 271mg | Carbs 32.8g | Fiber 6.4g | Sugar 7g | Protein 6.3g

Air Fried Okra

Prep Time: 10 minutes.
Cook Time: 13 minutes.
Serves: 2
Ingredients:
- ½ lb. okra pods sliced
- 1 teaspoon olive oil
- ¼ teaspoon salt
- ⅛ teaspoon black pepper

Preparation:
1. Preheat the Ninja Foodi Dual Zone Air Fryer to 350 degrees F.
2. Toss okra with olive oil, salt, and black pepper in a bowl.
3. Spread the okra in a single layer in the two crisper plates.
4. Return the crisper plate to the Ninja Foodi Dual Zone Air Fryer.
5. Choose the Air Fry mode for Zone 1 and set the temperature to 375 degrees F and the time to 13 minutes.
6. Select the "MATCH" button to copy the settings for Zone 2.
7. Initiate cooking by pressing the START/STOP button.
8. Toss the okra once cooked halfway through, and resume cooking.
9. Serve warm.
Serving Suggestion: Serve with potato chips and bread slices.
Variation Tip: Sprinkle cornmeal before cooking for added crisp.
Nutritional Information Per Serving:
Calories 208 | Fat 5g |Sodium 1205mg | Carbs 34.1g | Fiber 7.8g | Sugar 2.5g | Protein 5.9g

Stuffed Tomatoes

Prep Time: 12 Minutes
Cook Time: 8 Minutes
Serves: 2
Ingredients:
• 2 cups brown rice, cooked
• 1 cup tofu, grilled and chopped
• 4 large red tomatoes
• 4 tablespoons basil, chopped
• ¼ tablespoon olive oil
• Salt and black pepper, to taste
• 2 tablespoons lemon juice
• 1 teaspoon red chili powder
• ½ cup Parmesan cheese
Preparation:
1. Take a large bowl and mix rice, tofu, basil, olive oil, salt, black pepper, lemon juice, and chili powder.
2. Core the center of the tomatoes.
3. Fill the cavity with the rice mixture.
4. Top them off with the cheese sprinkle.
5. Divide the tomatoes into two air fryer baskets.
6. Turn zone 1 to AIR FRY mode for 8 minutes at 400 degrees F.
7. Select the MATCH button for zone 2.
8. Serve and enjoy.
Serving Suggestion: Serve it with Greek yogurt
Variation Tip: Use canola oil instead of olive oil
Nutritional Information Per Serving:
Calories 1034| Fat 24.2g| Sodium 527mg | Carbs 165g | Fiber 12.1g | Sugar 1.2g | Protein 43.9g

Kale and Spinach Chips

Prep Time: 12 Minutes
Cook Time: 6 Minutes
Serves: 2
Ingredients:
• 2 cups spinach, torn in pieces and stem removed
• 2 cups kale, torn in pieces, stems removed
• 1 tablespoon olive oil
• Sea salt, to taste
• ⅓ cup Parmesan cheese
Preparation:
1. Take a bowl and add spinach to it.
2. Take another bowl and add kale to it.
3. Season both of them with olive oil and sea salt.

4. Add the kale to the zone 1 basket and spinach to the zone 2 basket.
5. Select AIR FRY mode for zone 1 at 350 degrees F for 6 minutes.
6. Set zone 2 to AIR FRY mode at 350 degrees F for 5 minutes.
7. Once done, take out the crispy chips and sprinkle Parmesan cheese on top.
8. Serve and Enjoy.
Serving Suggestion: Serve with baked potato
Variation Tip: Use canola oil instead of olive oil
Nutritional Information Per Serving:
Calories 166| Fat 11.1g| Sodium 355mg | Carbs 8.1g | Fiber 1.7 g | Sugar 0.1g | Protein 8.2g

Mixed Air Fry Veggies

Prep Time: 15 Minutes
Cook Time: 25 Minutes
Serves: 4
Ingredients:
• 2 cups carrots, cubed
• 2 cups potatoes, cubed
• 2 cups shallots, cubed
• 2 cups zucchini, diced
• 2 cups yellow squash, cubed
• Salt and black pepper, to taste
• 1 tablespoon Italian seasoning
• 2 tablespoons ranch seasoning
• 4 tablespoons olive oil
Preparation:
1. Take a large bowl and add all the veggies to it.
2. Season the veggies with salt, pepper, Italian seasoning, ranch seasoning, and olive oil
3. Toss all the Ingredients: well.
4. Divide the veggies into both the baskets of the air fryer.
5. Set zone 1 basket to AIR FRY mode at 360 degrees F for 25 minutes.
6. Select the MATCH button for the zone 2 basket.
7. Once it is cooked and done, serve, and enjoy.
Serving Suggestion: Serve it with rice
Variation Tip: None
Nutritional Information Per Serving:
Calories 275| Fat 15.3g| Sodium 129 mg | Carbs 33g | Fiber 3.8g | Sugar 5g | Protein 4.4g

Green Beans with Baked Potatoes

Prep Time: 15 Minutes
Cook Time: 45 Minutes
Serves: 2

Ingredients:
- 2 cups green beans
- 2 large potatoes, cubed
- 3 tablespoons olive oil
- 1 teaspoon seasoned salt
- ½ teaspoon chili powder
- ⅛ teaspoon garlic powder
- ¼ teaspoon onion powder

Preparation:
1. Take a large bowl and pour olive oil into it.
2. Add all the seasoning in the olive oil and whisk it well.
3. Toss the green beans in and mix well and then transfer to zone 1 basket of the air fryer.
4. Season the potatoes with the oil seasoning and add them to the zone 2 basket.
5. Press the Sync button.
6. Once the cooking cycle is complete, take out and serve.

Serving Suggestion: Serve with rice
Variation Tip: Use canola oil instead of olive oil
Nutritional Information Per Serving:
Calories 473 | Fat 21.6g | Sodium 796mg | Carbs 66.6g | Fiber 12.9g | Sugar 6g | Protein 8.4g

Brussels Sprouts

Prep Time: 15 Minutes
Cook Time: 20 Minutes
Serves: 2

Ingredients:
- 2 pounds Brussels sprouts
- 2 tablespoons avocado oil
- Salt and pepper, to taste
- 1 cup pine nuts, roasted

Preparation:
1. Trim the bottom of the Brussels sprouts.
2. Take a bowl and combine the avocado oil, salt, and black pepper.
3. Toss the Brussels sprouts into the bowl and mix well.

4. Divide the mixture into both air fryer baskets.
5. For zone 1 set to AIR FRY mode for 20 minutes at 390 degrees F.
6. Select the MATCH button for the zone 2 basket.
7. Once the Brussels sprouts get crisp and tender, take out and serve.

Serving Suggestion: Serve with rice
Variation Tip: Use olive oil instead of avocado oil
Nutritional Information Per Serving:
Calories 672| Fat 50g| Sodium 115mg | Carbs 51g | Fiber 20.2g | Sugar 12.3g | Protein 25g

Fried Asparagus

Prep Time: 5 minutes
Cook Time: 6 minutes
Serves: 4

Ingredients:
- ¼ cup mayonnaise
- 4 teaspoons olive oil
- 1½ teaspoons grated lemon zest
- 1 garlic clove, minced
- ½ teaspoon pepper
- ¼ teaspoon seasoned salt
- 1-pound fresh asparagus, trimmed
- 2 tablespoons shredded parmesan cheese
- Lemon wedges (optional)

Preparation:
1. In a large bowl, combine the first 6 Ingredients:.
2. Add the asparagus; toss to coat.
3. Put a crisper plate in both drawers. Put the asparagus in a single layer in each drawer. Top with the parmesan cheese. Place the drawers into the unit.
4. Select zone 1, then AIR FRY, then set the temperature to 375°F with a 6-minute timer. To match zone 2 settings to zone 1, choose MATCH. To begin, select START/STOP.
5. Remove the asparagus from the drawers after the timer has finished.

Serving Suggestion: Serve with lemon wedges.
Variation Tip: You can use green beans instead.
Nutritional Information Per Serving:
Calories 156 | Fat 15g | Sodium 214mg | Carbs 3g | Fiber 1g | Sugar 1g | Protein 2g

Mushroom Roll-Ups

Prep Time: 30 minutes
Cook Time: 10 minutes
Serves: 10
Ingredients:
• 2 tablespoons extra virgin olive oil
• 8 ounces large portobello mushrooms (gills discarded), finely chopped
• 1 teaspoon dried oregano
• 1 teaspoon dried thyme
• ½ teaspoon crushed red pepper flakes
• ¼ teaspoon salt
• 8 ounces cream cheese, softened
• 4 ounces whole-milk ricotta cheese
• 10 flour tortillas (8-inch)
• Cooking spray
• Chutney, for serving (optional)
Preparation:
1. Heat the oil in a pan over medium heat. Add the mushrooms and cook for 4 minutes. Sauté until the mushrooms are browned, about 4-6 minutes, with the oregano, thyme, pepper flakes, and salt. Cool.
2. Combine the cheeses in a mixing bowl; fold in the mushrooms until thoroughly combined.
3. On the bottom center of each tortilla, spread 3 tablespoons of the mushroom mixture. Tightly roll up each tortilla and secure with toothpicks.
4. Place a crisper plate in each drawer. Put the roll-ups in a single layer in each. Insert the drawers into the unit.
5. Select zone 1, then AIR FRY, then set the temperature to 400°F with a 10-minute timer. To match zone 2 settings to zone 1, choose MATCH. To begin, select START/STOP.
6. Remove the roll-ups from the drawers after the timer has finished. When they have cooled enough to handle, discard the toothpicks.
7. Serve and enjoy!
Serving Suggestion: Serve the roll-ups with chutney.
Variation Tip: You can use gluten-free tortillas.
Nutritional Information Per Serving:
Calories 291 | Fat 16g | Sodium 380mg | Carbs 31g | Fiber 2g | Sugar 2g | Protein 8g

Beets With Orange Gremolata and Goat's Cheese

Prep Time: 25 minutes
Cook Time: 45 minutes
Serves: 12
Ingredients:
• 3 medium fresh golden beets (about 1 pound)
• 3 medium fresh beets (about 1 pound)
• 2 tablespoons lime juice
• 2 tablespoons orange juice
• ½ teaspoon fine sea salt
• 1 tablespoon minced fresh parsley
• 1 tablespoon minced fresh sage
• 1 garlic clove, minced
• 1 teaspoon grated orange zest
• 3 tablespoons crumbled goat's cheese
• 2 tablespoons sunflower kernels
Preparation:
1. Scrub the beets and trim the tops by 1 inch.
2. Place the beets on a double thickness of heavy-duty foil (about 24 x 12 inches). Fold the foil around the beets, sealing tightly.
3. Place a crisper plate in both drawers. Put the beets in a single layer in each drawer. Insert the drawers into the unit.
4. Select zone 1, then AIR FRY, then set the temperature to 360°F with a 45-minute timer. To match zone 2 settings to zone 1, choose MATCH. To begin, select START/STOP.
5. Remove the beets from the drawers after the timer has finished. Peel, halve, and slice them when they're cool enough to handle. Place them in a serving bowl.
6. Toss in the lime juice, orange juice, and salt to coat. Sprinkle the beets with the parsley, sage, garlic, and orange zest. The sunflower kernels and goat's cheese go on top.
Serving Suggestion: Serve warm or cooled.
Variation Tip: You can use lemon zest.
Nutritional Information Per Serving:
Calories 481 | Fat 20g | Sodium 1162mg | Carbs 56g | Fiber 4g | Sugar 9g | Protein 19g

Fried Avocado Tacos

Prep Time: 30 minutes
Cook Time: 10 minutes
Serves: 4
Ingredients:
For the sauce:
• 2 cups shredded fresh kale or coleslaw mix
• ¼ cup minced fresh cilantro
• ¼ cup plain Greek yogurt
• 2 tablespoons lime juice
• 1 teaspoon honey
• ¼ teaspoon salt
• ¼ teaspoon ground chipotle pepper
• ¼ teaspoon pepper
For the tacos:
• 1 large egg, beaten
• ¼ cup cornmeal
• ½ teaspoon salt
• ½ teaspoon garlic powder
• ½ teaspoon ground chipotle pepper
• 2 medium avocados, peeled and sliced
• Cooking spray
• 8 flour tortillas or corn tortillas (6 inches), heated up
• 1 medium tomato, chopped
• Crumbled queso fresco (optional)
Preparation:
1. Combine the first 8 Ingredients: in a bowl. Cover and refrigerate until serving.
2. Place the egg in a shallow bowl. In another shallow bowl, mix the cornmeal, salt, garlic powder, and chipotle pepper.
3. Dip the avocado slices in the egg, then into the cornmeal mixture, gently patting to help adhere.
4. Place a crisper plate in both drawers. Put the avocado slices in the drawers in a single layer. Insert the drawers into the unit.
5. Select zone 1, then AIR FRY, then set the temperature to 360°F with a 6-minute timer. To match zone 2 settings to zone 1, choose MATCH. To begin, select START/STOP.
6. Put the avocado slices, prepared sauce, tomato, and queso fresco in the tortillas and serve.
Serving Suggestion: Add some more chopped cilantro.

Variation Tip: You can use panko breadcrumbs instead of cornmeal.
Nutritional Information Per Serving:
Calories 407 | Fat 21g | Sodium 738mg | Carbs 48g | Fiber 4g | Sugar 9g | Protein 9g

Buffalo Bites

Prep Time: 10 minutes
Cook Time: 30 minutes
Serves: 6
Ingredients:
For the bites:
• 1 small cauliflower head, cut into florets
• 2 tablespoons olive oil
• 3 tablespoons buffalo wing sauce
• 3 tablespoons butter, melted
For the dip:
• 1½ cups 2% cottage cheese
• ¼ cup fat-free plain Greek yogurt
• ¼ cup crumbled blue cheese
• 1 sachet ranch salad dressing mix
• Celery sticks (optional)
Preparation:
1. In a large bowl, combine the cauliflower and oil; toss to coat.
2. Place a crisper plate in each drawer. Put the coated cauliflower florets in each drawer in a single layer. Place the drawers in the unit.
3. Select zone 1, then AIR FRY, then set the temperature to 360°F with a 15-minute timer. To match zone 2 settings to zone 1, choose MATCH. To begin, select START/STOP.
4. Remove the cauliflower from the drawers after the timer has finished.
5. Combine the buffalo sauce and melted butter in a large mixing bowl. Put in the cauliflower and toss to coat. Place on a serving dish and serve.
6. Combine the dip Ingredients: in a small bowl. Serve with the cauliflower and celery sticks, if desired.
Serving Suggestion: Serve with the dipping sauce.
Variation Tip: You can use buttermilk.
Nutritional Information Per Serving:
Calories 203 | Fat 13g | Sodium 1470mg | Carbs 13g | Fiber 4g | Sugar 1g | Protein 9g

Garlic Potato Wedges in Air Fryer

Prep Time: 10 Minutes
Cook Time: 23 Minutes
Serves: 2
Ingredients:
• 4 medium potatoes, peeled and cut into wedges
• 4 tablespoons butter
• 1 teaspoon chopped cilantro
• 1 cup plain flour
• 1 teaspoon garlic, minced
• Salt and black pepper, to taste
Preparation:
1. Soak the potato wedges in cold water for about 30 minutes.
2. Drain and pat dry with a paper towel.
3. Boil water in a large pot and boil the wedges for 3 minutes and place on a paper towel.
4. In a bowl, mix garlic, melted butter, salt, pepper, and cilantro.
5. Add the flour to a separate bowl along with the salt and black pepper.
6. Add water to the flour so it gets a runny in texture.
7. Coat the potatoes with the flour mixture and divide them into two foil tins.
8. Place the foil tins in each air fryer basket.
9. Set the zone 1 basket to AIR FRY mode at 390 degrees F for 20 minutes.
10. Select the MATCH button for the zone 2 basket.
11. Once done, serve and enjoy.
Serving Suggestion: Serve with ketchup
Variation Tip: Use olive oil instead of butter
Nutritional Information Per Serving:
Calories 727| Fat 24.1g| Sodium 191mg | Carbs 115.1g | Fiber 12g | Sugar 5.1g | Protein 14g

Sweet Potatoes with Honey Butter

Prep Time: 15 minutes.
Cook Time: 40 minutes.
Serves: 4
Ingredients:
• 4 sweet potatoes, scrubbed
• 1 teaspoon oil
Honey Butter
• 4 tablespoons unsalted butter
• 1 tablespoon Honey
• 2 teaspoons hot sauce
• ¼ teaspoon salt
Preparation:
1. Rub the sweet potatoes with oil and place two potatoes in each crisper plate.
2. Return the crisper plate to the Ninja Foodi Dual Zone Air Fryer.
3. Choose the Air Fry mode for Zone 1 and set the temperature to 400 degrees F and the time to 40 minutes.
4. Select the "MATCH" button to copy the settings for Zone 2.
5. Initiate cooking by pressing the START/STOP button.
6. Flip the potatoes once cooked halfway through, then resume cooking.
7. Mix butter with hot sauce, honey, and salt in a bowl.
8. When the potatoes are done, cut a slit on top and make a well with a spoon
9. Pour the honey butter in each potato jacket.
10. Serve.
Serving Suggestion: Serve with sautéed vegetables and salad.
Variation Tip: Sprinkle crumbled bacon and parsley on top.
Nutritional Information Per Serving:
Calories 288 | Fat 6.9g |Sodium 761mg | Carbs 46g | Fiber 4g | Sugar 12g | Protein 9.6g

Cheesy Potatoes with Asparagus

Prep Time: 15 Minutes
Cook Time: 35 Minutes
Serves: 2

Ingredients:
• 1-½ pounds russet potato, wedges or cut in half
• 2 teaspoons mixed herbs
• 2 teaspoons chili flakes
• 2 cups asparagus
• 1 cup chopped onion
• 1 tablespoon Dijon mustard
• ¼ cup fresh cream
• 1 teaspoon olive oil
• 2 tablespoons butter
• ½ teaspoon salt and black pepper
• Water as required
• ½ cup Parmesan cheese

Preparation:
1. Take a bowl and add asparagus and sweet potato wedges to it.
2. Season it with salt, black pepper, and olive oil.
3. Add the potato wedges to the zone 1 air fryer basket and asparagus to the zone 2 basket.
4. Set zone 1 to AIR FRY mode at 390 degrees F for 12 minutes.
5. Set the zone 2 basket to AIR FRY mode at 390 degrees F for 30-35 minutes. Click Sync button
6. Meanwhile, take a skillet and add butter and sauté the onion in it for a few minutes.
7. Then add salt and Dijon mustard and chili flakes, Parmesan cheese, and fresh cream.
8. Once the veggies are cooked take them out and drizzle the cream mixture on top.

Serving Suggestion: Serve with rice
Variation Tip: Use olive oil instead of butter
Nutritional Information Per Serving:
Calories 251| Fat 11g | Sodium 279mg | Carbs 31.1g | Fiber 5g | Sugar 4.1g | Protein 9g

Garlic-Rosemary Brussels Sprouts

Prep Time: 5 minutes
Cook Time: 15 minutes
Serves: 4

Ingredients:
• 3 tablespoons olive oil
• 2 garlic cloves, minced
• ½ teaspoon salt
• ¼ teaspoon pepper
• 1-pound Brussels sprouts, trimmed and halved
• ½ cup panko breadcrumbs
• 1½ teaspoons minced fresh rosemary

Preparation:
1. Place the first 4 Ingredients: in a small microwave-safe bowl; microwave on high for 30 seconds.
2. Toss the Brussels sprouts in 2 tablespoons of the microwaved mixture.
3. Place a crisper plate in each drawer. Put the sprouts in a single layer in each drawer. Insert the drawers into the units.
4. Select zone 1, then AIR FRY, then set the temperature to 360°F with a 6-minute timer. To match zone 2 settings to zone 1, choose MATCH. To begin, select START/STOP.
5. Remove the sprouts from the drawers after the timer has finished.
6. Toss the breadcrumbs with the rosemary and remaining oil mixture; sprinkle over the sprouts.
7. Continue cooking (same settings) until the crumbs are browned, and the sprouts are tender (3 to 5 minutes). Serve immediately.

Serving Suggestion: Serve with a side salad.
Variation Tip: Use cracker crumbs instead of breadcrumbs.
Nutritional Information Per Serving:
Calories 164 | Fat 11g | Sodium 342mg | Carbs 15g | Fiber 3g | Sugar 4g | Protein 5g

Herb and Lemon Cauliflower

Prep Time: 5 minutes
Cook Time: 10 minutes
Serves: 4
Ingredients:
• 1 medium cauliflower, cut into florets (about 6 cups)
• 4 tablespoons olive oil, divided
• ¼ cup minced fresh parsley
• 1 tablespoon minced fresh rosemary
• 1 tablespoon minced fresh thyme
• 1 teaspoon grated lemon zest
• 2 tablespoons lemon juice
• ½ teaspoon salt
• ¼ teaspoon crushed red pepper flakes
Preparation:
1. In a large bowl, combine the cauliflower florets and 2 tablespoons olive oil; toss to coat.
2. Put a crisper plate in both drawers, then put the cauliflower in a single layer in each. Insert the drawers into the unit.
3. Select zone 1, then AIR FRY, then set the temperature to 350°F with a 10-minute timer. To match zone 2 settings to zone 1, choose MATCH. To begin, select START/STOP.
4. Remove the cauliflower from the drawers after the timer has finished.
5. In a small bowl, combine the remaining Ingredients:. Stir in the remaining 2 tablespoons of oil.
6. Transfer the cauliflower to a large bowl and drizzle with the herb mixture. Toss to combine.
Serving Suggestion: Serve with a side salad.
Variation Tip: You can use broccoli instead.
Nutritional Information Per Serving:
Calories 161 | Fat 14g | Sodium 342mg | Carbs 8g | Fiber 3g | Sugar 3g | Protein 3g

Pepper Poppers

Prep Time: 15 minutes
Cook Time: 20 minutes
Serves: 24
Ingredients:
• 8 ounces cream cheese, softened
• ¾ cup shredded cheddar cheese
• ¾ cup shredded Monterey Jack cheese
• 6 bacon strips, cooked and crumbled
• ¼ teaspoon salt
• ¼ teaspoon garlic powder
• ¼ teaspoon chili powder
• ¼ teaspoon smoked paprika
• 1-pound fresh jalapeño peppers, halved lengthwise and deseeded
• ½ cup dry breadcrumbs
• Sour cream, French onion dip, or ranch salad dressing (optional)
Preparation:
1. In a large bowl, combine the cheeses, bacon, and seasonings; mix well. Spoon 1½ to 2 tablespoons of the mixture into each pepper half. Roll them in the breadcrumbs.
2. Place a crisper plate in each drawer. Put the prepared peppers in a single layer in each drawer. Insert the drawers into the unit.
3. Select zone 1, then AIR FRY, then set the temperature to 360°F with a 20-minute timer. To match zone 2 settings to zone 1, choose MATCH. To begin, select START/STOP.
4. Remove the peppers from the drawers after the timer has finished.
Serving Suggestion: Serve with sour cream, French onion dip, or ranch dressing.
Variation Tip: You can use bell peppers instead.
Nutritional Information Per Serving:
Calories 81 | Fat 6g | Sodium 145mg | Carbs 3g | Fiber 4g | Sugar 1g | Protein 3g

Fried Olives

Prep Time: 15 minutes.
Cook Time: 9 minutes.
Serves: 6

Ingredients:
• 2 cups blue cheese stuffed olives, drained
• ½ cup all-purpose flour
• 1 cup panko breadcrumbs
• ½ teaspoon garlic powder
• 1 pinch oregano
• 2 eggs

Preparation:
1. Mix flour with oregano and garlic powder in a bowl and beat two eggs in another bowl.
2. Spread panko breadcrumbs in a bowl.
3. Coat all the olives with the flour mixture, dip in the eggs and then coat with the panko breadcrumbs.
4. As you coat the olives, place them in the two crisper plates in a single layer, then spray them with cooking oil.
5. Return the crisper plates to the Ninja Foodi Dual Zone Air Fryer.
6. Choose the Air Fry mode for Zone 1 and set the temperature to 375 degrees F and the time to 9 minutes.
7. Select the "MATCH" button to copy the settings for Zone 2.
8. Initiate cooking by pressing the START/STOP button.
9. Flip the olives once cooked halfway through, then resume cooking.
10. Serve.

Serving Suggestion: Serve with red chunky salsa or chili sauce.
Variation Tip: Use crushed cornflakes for breading to have extra crispiness.
Nutritional Information Per Serving:
Calories 166 | Fat 3.2g |Sodium 437mg | Carbs 28.8g | Fiber 1.8g | Sugar 2.7g | Protein 5.8g

Garlic Herbed Baked Potatoes

Prep Time: 25 Minutes
Cook Time: 45 Minutes
Serves: 4

Ingredients:
• 4 large baking potatoes
• Salt and black pepper, to taste
• 2 teaspoons avocado oil

Cheese Ingredients:
• 2 cups sour cream
• 1 teaspoon garlic clove, minced
• 1 teaspoon fresh dill
• 2 teaspoons chopped chives
• Salt and black pepper, to taste
• 2 teaspoons Worcestershire sauce

Preparation:
1. Pierce the skin of the potatoes with a fork.
2. Season the potatoes with olive oil, salt, and black pepper.
3. Divide the potatoes into the air fryer baskets.
4. Now press 1 for zone 1 and set it to AIR FRY mode at 350 degrees F, for 45 minutes.
5. Select the MATCH button for zone 2.
6. Meanwhile, take a bowl and mix all the cheese Ingredients: together.
7. Once the cooking cycle is complete, take out the potatoes and make a slit in-between each one.
8. Add the cheese mixture in the cavity and serve it hot.

Serving Suggestion: Serve with gravy
Variation Tip: None
Nutritional Information Per Serving:
Calories 382| Fat 24.6g| Sodium 107mg | Carbs 36.2g | Fiber 2.5g | Sugar 2g | Protein 7.3g

Chapter 4 Fish and Seafood Recipes

Salmon Nuggets

Prep Time: 15 minutes.
Cook Time: 15 minutes.
Serves: 4
Ingredients:
• ⅓ cup maple syrup
• ¼ teaspoon dried chipotle pepper
• 1 pinch sea salt
• 1 ½ cups croutons
• 1 large egg
• 1 (1 pound) skinless salmon fillet, cut into 1 ½-inch chunk
• cooking spray
Preparation:
1. Mix chipotle powder, maple syrup, and salt in a saucepan and cook on a simmer for 5 minutes.
2. Crush the croutons in a food processor and transfer to a bowl.
3. Beat egg in another shallow bowl.
4. Season the salmon chunks with sea salt.
5. Dip the salmon in the egg, then coat with breadcrumbs.
6. Divide the coated salmon chunks in the two crisper plates.
7. Return the crisper plate to the Ninja Foodi Dual Zone Air Fryer.
8. Select the Air Fry mode for Zone 1 and set the temperature to 390 degrees F and the time to 10 minutes.
9. Press the "MATCH" button to copy the settings for Zone 2.
10. Initiate cooking by pressing the START/STOP button.
11. Flip the chunks once cooked halfway through, then resume cooking.
12. Pour the maple syrup on top and serve warm.
Serving Suggestion: Serve with creamy dip and crispy fries.
Variation Tip: Use crushed cornflakes for breading to have extra crispiness.
Nutritional Information Per Serving:
Calories 275 | Fat 1.4g |Sodium 582mg | Carbs 31.5g | Fiber 1.1g | Sugar 0.1g | Protein 29.8g

Beer Battered Fish Fillet

Prep Time: 18 Minutes
Cook Time: 14 Minutes
Serves: 2
Ingredients:
• 1 cup all-purpose flour
• 4 tablespoons cornstarch
• 1 teaspoon baking soda
• 8 ounces beer
• 2 egg beaten
• 1 teaspoon smoked Paprika
• 1 teaspoon salt
• ¼ teaspoon freshly ground black pepper
• ¼ teaspoon cayenne pepper
• 2 cod fillets, 1½-inches thick, cut into 4 pieces
• Oil spray, for greasing
Preparation:
1. Take a large bowl and combine 1 cup flour, baking soda, cornstarch, and salt.
2. In a separate bowl, beat the eggs along with the beer.
3. In a shallow dish, mix paprika, salt, pepper, and cayenne pepper.
4. Dry the codfish fillets with a paper towel.
5. Dip the fish into the eggs and coat them with the flour mixture.
6. Then dip it in the seasoning.
7. Grease the fillets with oil spray.
8. Divide the fillets between both zones.
9. Set zone 1 to AIR FRY mode at 400 degrees F for 14 minutes.
10. Select MATCH button for zone 2 basket.
11. Press START/STOP button and let them cook.
12. Once the cooking is done, serve the fish.
13. Enjoy it hot.
Serving Suggestion: Serve it with rice
Variation Tip: Use mild Paprika instead of smoked Paprika
Nutritional Information Per Serving:
Calories 1691| Fat 6.1g| Sodium 3976mg | Carbs 105.1 g | Fiber 3.4g | Sugar 15.6 g | Protein 270g

Honey Sriracha Mahi Mahi

Prep Time: 5 minutes
Cook Time: 7 minutes
Serves: 4

Ingredients:
- 3 pounds mahi-mahi
- 6 tablespoons honey
- 4 tablespoons sriracha
- Salt, to taste
- Cooking spray

Preparation:
1. In a small bowl, mix the sriracha sauce and honey. Mix well.
2. Season the fish with salt and pour the honey mixture over it. Let it sit at room temperature for 20 minutes.
3. Place a crisper plate in each drawer. Put the fish in a single layer in each. Insert the drawers into the unit.
4. Select zone 1, then AIR FRY, then set the temperature to 400°F with a 7-minute timer. To match zone 2 settings to zone 1, choose MATCH. To begin, select START/STOP.
5. Remove the fish from the drawers after the timer has finished.

Serving Suggestion: Serve with cauliflower rice.
Variation Tip: You can use cod or salmon instead.
Nutritional Information Per Serving:
Calories 581 | Fat 22g | Sodium 495mg | Carbs 26g | Fiber 4g | Sugar 26g | Protein 68g

Honey Teriyaki Tilapia

Prep Time: 5 minutes
Cook Time: 10 minutes
Serves: 4

Ingredients:
- 8 tablespoons low-sodium teriyaki sauce
- 3 tablespoons honey
- 2 garlic cloves, minced
- 2 tablespoons extra virgin olive oil
- 3 pieces tilapia (each cut into 2 pieces)

Preparation:
1. Combine all the first 4 Ingredients: to make the marinade.
2. Pour the marinade over the tilapia and let it sit for 20 minutes.

3. Place a crisper plate in each drawer. Place the tilapia in the drawers. Insert the drawers into the unit.
4. Select zone 1, then AIR FRY, then set the temperature to 360°F with a 10-minute timer. To match zone 2 settings to zone 1, choose MATCH. To begin, select START/STOP.
5. Remove the tilapia from the drawers after the timer has finished.

Serving Suggestion: Serve over a bed of rice.
Variation Tip: You can use maple syrup instead of honey.
Nutritional Information Per Serving:
Calories 350 | Fat 16.4g | Sodium 706mg | Carbs 19.3g | Fiber 0.1g | Sugar 19g | Protein 29.3g

Salmon with Green Beans

Prep Time: 12 Minutes
Cook Time: 18 Minutes
Serves: 1

Ingredients:
- 1 salmon fillet, 2 inches thick
- 2 teaspoons olive oil
- 2 teaspoons smoked Paprika
- Salt and black pepper, to taste
- 1 cup green beans
- Oil spray, for greasing

Preparation:
1. Grease the green beans with oil spray and add them to the zone 1 basket.
2. Rub the salmon fillet with olive oil, smoked Paprika, salt, and black pepper.
3. Put the salmon fillet in the zone 2 basket.
4. Set the zone 1 basket to AIR FRY mode at 350 degrees F for 18 minutes.
5. Set the zone 2 basket to 390 degrees F for 16-18 minutes.
6. Hit the Sync button so that they both finish at the same time.
7. Once done, take out the salmon and green beans, transfer them to the serving plates and enjoy.

Serving Suggestion: Serve it with ranch
Variation Tip: Use any other green vegetable of your choice
Nutritional Information Per Serving:
Calories 367| Fat 22 g| Sodium 87mg | Carbs 10.2g | Fiber 5.3g | Sugar 2g | Protein 37.2g

Frozen Breaded Fish Fillet

Prep Time: 15 Minutes
Cook Time: 12 Minutes
Serves: 2

Ingredients:
• 4 frozen breaded fish fillets
• Oil spray, for greasing
• 1 cup mayonnaise

Preparation:
1. Take the frozen fish fillets out of the bag and place them in both baskets of the air fryer.
2. Lightly grease them with oil spray.
3. Set the zone 1 basket to 380 degrees F for 12 minutes.
4. Select the MATCH button for the zone 2 basket.
5. Hit the START/STOP button to start cooking.
6. Once the cooking is done, serve the fish hot with mayonnaise.

Serving Suggestion: Serve it with salad and rice
Variation Tip: Use olive oil instead of butter
Nutritional Information Per Serving:
Calories 921| Fat 61.5g| Sodium 1575mg | Carbs 69g | Fiber 2g | Sugar 9.5g | Protein 29.1g

Salmon with Broccoli and Cheese

Prep Time: 15 Minutes
Cook Time: 18 Minutes
Serves: 2

Ingredients:
• 2 cups broccoli
• ½ cup butter, melted
• Salt and pepper, to taste
• Oil spray, for greasing
• 1 cup grated Cheddar cheese
• 1 pound salmon, fillets

Preparation:
1. Take a bowl and add broccoli to it.
2. Add salt and black pepper and spray the broccoli with oil.
3. Put the broccoli in the air fryer zone 1 basket.
4. Rub the salmon fillets with salt, black pepper, and butter.
5. Place them into zone 2 basket.
6. Set zone 1 to AIR FRY mode for 5 minters at 400 degrees F.
7. Set zone 2 to AIR FRY mode for 18 minutes at 390 degrees F.
8. Sprinkle the grated cheese on top of the salmon and serve.

Serving Suggestion: Serve with rice and baked potato
Variation Tip: Use olive oil instead of butter
Nutritional Information Per Serving:
Calories 966 | Fat 79.1g| Sodium 808mg | Carbs 6.8g | Fiber 2.4g | Sugar 1.9g | Protein 61.2g

Spicy Fish Fillet with Onion Rings

Prep Time: 10 Minutes
Cook Time: 12 Minutes
Serves:1

Ingredients:
• 300 grams onion rings, frozen and packed
• 1 codfish fillet, 8 ounces
• Salt and black pepper, to taste
• 1 teaspoon lemon juice
• Oil spray, for greasing

Preparation:
1. Place the frozen onion rings in zone 1 basket of the air fryer.
2. Pat dry the fish fillets with a paper towel and season them with salt, black pepper, and lemon juice.
3. Grease the fillet with oil spray.
4. Put the fish in the zone 2 basket.
5. Use MAX CRISP for zone 1 at 240 degrees F for 9 minutes.
6. Set zone 2 to MAX CRISP mode and set it to 210 degrees F for 12 minutes.
7. Press Sync and press START/STOP button.
8. Once done, serve hot.

Serving Suggestion: Serve with buffalo sauce
Variation Tip: None
Nutritional Information Per Serving:
Calories 666| Fat23.5g| Sodium 911mg | Carbs 82g | Fiber 8.8g | Sugar 17.4g | Protein 30.4g

Fish Tacos

Prep Time: 10 minutes
Cook Time: 30 minutes
Serves: 5
Ingredients:
• 1 pound firm white fish such as cod, haddock, pollock, halibut, or walleye
• ¾ cup gluten-free flour blend
• 3 eggs
• 1 cup gluten-free panko breadcrumbs
• 1 teaspoon garlic powder
• 1 teaspoon onion powder
• 1 teaspoon cumin
• 1 teaspoon lemon pepper
• 1 teaspoon red chili flakes
• 1 teaspoon kosher salt, divided
• 1 teaspoon pepper, divided
• Cooking oil spray
• 1 package corn tortillas
• Toppings such as tomatoes, avocado, cabbage, radishes, jalapenos, salsa, or hot sauce (optional)
Preparation:
1. Dry the fish with paper towels. (Make sure to thaw the fish if it's frozen.) Depending on the size of the fillets, cut the fish in half or thirds.
2. On both sides of the fish pieces, liberally season with salt and pepper.
3. Put the flour in a dish.
4. In a separate bowl, crack the eggs and whisk them together until well blended.
5. Put the panko breadcrumbs in another bowl. Add the garlic powder, onion powder, cumin, lemon pepper, and red chili flakes. Add salt and pepper to taste. Stir until everything is well blended.
6. Each piece of fish should be dipped in the flour, then the eggs, and finally in the breadcrumb mixture. Make sure that each piece is completely coated.
7. Put a crisper plate in each drawer. Arrange the fish pieces in a single layer in each drawer. Insert the drawers into the unit.
8. Select zone 1, then AIR FRY, then set the temperature to 360°F with a 20-minute timer. To match zone 2 settings to zone 1, choose MATCH. To begin, select START/STOP.
9. Remove the fish from the drawers after the timer has finished. Place the crispy fish on warmed tortillas.

Serving Suggestion: Serve the fish tacos topped with toppings and sauce of your choice.
Variation Tip: You can use all-purpose flour.
Nutritional Information Per Serving:
Calories 534 | Fat 18g | Sodium 679mg | Carbs 63g | Fiber 8g | Sugar 3g | Protein 27g

Bacon-Wrapped Shrimp

Prep Time: 45 minutes
Cook Time: 10 minutes
Serves: 8
Ingredients:
• 24 jumbo raw shrimp, deveined with tail on, fresh or thawed from frozen
• 8 slices bacon, cut into thirds
• 1 tablespoon olive oil
• 1 teaspoon paprika
• 1–2 cloves minced garlic
• 1 tablespoon finely chopped fresh parsley
Preparation:
1. Combine the olive oil, paprika, garlic, and parsley in a small bowl.
2. If necessary, peel the raw shrimp, leaving the tails on.
3. Add the shrimp to the oil mixture. Toss to coat well.
4. Wrap a piece of bacon around the middle of each shrimp and place seam-side down on a small baking dish.
5. Refrigerate for 30 minutes before cooking.
6. Place a crisper plate in each drawer. Put the shrimp in a single layer in each drawer. Insert the drawers into the unit.
7. Select zone 1, then AIR FRY, then set the temperature to 360°F with a 10-minute timer. To match zone 2 settings to zone 1, choose MATCH. To begin, select START/STOP.
8. Remove the shrimp from the drawers when the cooking time is over.
Serving Suggestion: Serve with a sauce of your choice.
Variation Tip: You can use ham slices instead of bacon.
Nutritional Information Per Serving:
Calories 479 | Fat 15.7g | Sodium 949mg | Carbs 0.6g | Fiber 0.1g | Sugar 0g | Protein 76.1g

Roasted Salmon and Parmesan Asparagus

Prep Time: 10 minutes
Cook Time: 27 minutes
Serves: 4
Ingredients:
• 2 tablespoons Montreal steak seasoning
• 3 tablespoons brown sugar
• 3 uncooked salmon fillets (6 ounces each)
• 2 tablespoons canola oil, divided
• 1-pound asparagus, ends trimmed
• Kosher salt, as desired
• Ground black pepper, as desired
• ¼ cup shredded parmesan cheese, divided
Preparation:
1. Combine the steak spice and brown sugar in a small bowl.
2. Brush 1 tablespoon of oil over the salmon fillets, then thoroughly coat with the sugar mixture.
3. Toss the asparagus with the remaining 1 tablespoon of oil, salt, and pepper in a mixing bowl.
4. Place a crisper plate in both drawers. Put the fillets skin-side down in the zone 1 drawer, then place the drawer in the unit. Insert the zone 2 drawer into the device after placing the asparagus in it.
5. Select zone 1, then ROAST, then set the temperature to 390°F with a 17-minute timer. To match the zone 2 settings to zone 1, choose MATCH. To begin cooking, press the START/STOP button.
6. When the zone 2 timer reaches 7 minutes, press START/STOP. Remove the zone 2 drawer from the unit. Flip the asparagus with silicone-tipped tongs. Re-insert the drawer into the unit. Continue cooking by pressing START/STOP.
7. When the zone 2 timer has reached 14 minutes, press START/STOP. Remove the zone 2 drawer from the unit. Sprinkle half the parmesan cheese over the asparagus, and mix lightly. Re-insert the drawer into the unit. Continue cooking by pressing START/STOP.
8. Transfer the fillets and asparagus to a serving plate once they've finished cooking. Serve with the remaining parmesan cheese on top of the asparagus.
Serving Suggestion: Serve with steamed rice.
Variation Tip: Use green beans instead of asparagus.
Nutritional Information Per Serving:
Calories 293 | Fat 15.8g | Sodium 203mg | Carbs 11.1g | Fiber 2.4g | Sugar 8.7g | Protein 29g

Seafood Shrimp Omelet

Prep Time: 20 Minutes
Cook Time: 15 Minutes
Serves: 2
Ingredients:
• 6 large shrimp, shells removed and chopped
• 6 eggs, beaten
• ½ tablespoon butter, melted
• 2 tablespoons green onions, sliced
• ⅓ cup mushrooms, chopped
• 1 pinch Paprika
• Salt and black pepper, to taste
• Oil spray, for greasing
Preparation:
1. In a large bowl, whisk the eggs and add the chopped shrimp, butter, green onions, mushrooms, paprika, salt, and black pepper.
2. Take two cake pans that fit inside the air fryer and grease them with oil spray.
3. Pour the egg mixture between the cake pans and place it in the air fryer baskets.
4. Set zone 1 to BAKE mode and set the temperature to 320 degrees F for 15 minutes.
5. Select the MATCH button to match the cooking time for the zone 2 basket.
6. Once the cooking cycle is complete, take out, and serve hot.
Serving Suggestion: Serve it with rice
Variation Tip: Use olive oil for greasing purposes
Nutritional Information Per Serving:
Calories 300 | Fat 17.5g| Sodium 368mg | Carbs 2.9g | Fiber 0.3g | Sugar 1.4 g | Protein 32.2g

Bang Bang Shrimp

Prep Time: 15 minutes
Cook Time: 20 minutes
Serves: 4

Ingredients:

For the shrimp:
- 1 cup corn starch
- Salt and pepper, to taste
- 2 pounds shrimp, peeled and deveined
- ½ to 1 cup buttermilk
- Cooking oil spray
- 1 large egg whisked with 1 teaspoon water

For the sauce:
- $1/3$ cup sweet Thai chili sauce
- ¼ cup sour cream
- ¼ cup mayonnaise
- 2 tablespoons buttermilk
- 1 tablespoon sriracha, or to taste
- Pinch dried dill weed

Preparation:
1. Season the corn starch with salt and pepper in a wide, shallow bowl.
2. In a large mixing bowl, toss the shrimp in the buttermilk to coat them.
3. Dredge the shrimp in the seasoned corn starch.
4. Brush with the egg wash after spraying with cooking oil.
5. Place a crisper plate in each drawer. Place the shrimp in a single layer in each. You may need to cook in batches.
6. Select zone 1, then AIR FRY, then set the temperature to 360°F with a 5-minute timer. To match zone 2 settings to zone 1, choose MATCH. To begin, select START/STOP.
7. Meanwhile, combine all the sauce Ingredients: together in a bowl.
8. Remove the shrimp when the cooking time is over.

Serving Suggestion: Serve the shrimp with the sauce on the side.

Variation Tip: You can use potato starch instead of corn starch.

Nutritional Information Per Serving:
Calories 415 | Fat 15g | Sodium 1875mg | Carbs 28g | Fiber 1g | Sugar 5g | Protein 38g

Scallops

Prep Time: 10 minutes
Cook Time: 5 minutes
Serves: 4

Ingredients:
- ½ cup Italian breadcrumbs
- ½ teaspoon garlic powder
- ¼ teaspoon salt
- ½ teaspoon black pepper
- 2 tablespoons butter, melted
- 1 pound sea scallops, rinsed and pat dry

Preparation:
1. Combine the breadcrumbs, garlic powder, salt, and pepper in a small bowl. Pour the melted butter into another shallow bowl.
2. Dredge each scallop in the melted butter, then roll it in the breadcrumb mixture until well covered.
3. Place a crisper plate in each drawer. Put the scallops in a single layer in each drawer. Insert the drawers into the unit.
4. Select zone 1, then AIR FRY, then set the temperature to 360°F with a 5-minute timer. To match zone 2 settings to zone 1, choose MATCH. To begin, select START/STOP.
5. Press START/STOP to pause the unit when the timer reaches 3 minutes. Remove the drawers. Use tongs to carefully flip the scallops over. To resume cooking, re-insert the drawers into the unit and press START/STOP.
6. Remove the scallops from the drawers after the timer has finished.

Serving Suggestion: Serve with lemon wedges and a side salad.

Variation Tip: You can add some chopped parsley.

Nutritional Information Per Serving:
Calories 81 | Fat 6g | Sodium 145mg | Carbs 3g | Fiber 4g | Sugar 1g | Protein 3g

Codfish with Herb Vinaigrette

Prep Time: 15 Minutes
Cook Time: 16 Minutes
Serves: 2
Ingredients:
Vinaigrette Ingredients:
• ½ cup parsley leaves
• 1 cup basil leaves
• ½ cup mint leaves
• 2 tablespoons thyme leaves
• ¼ teaspoon red pepper flakes
• 2 cloves garlic
• 4 tablespoons red wine vinegar
• ¼ cup olive oil
• Salt, to taste
Other Ingredients:
• 1.5 pounds fish fillets, codfish
• 2 tablespoons olive oil
• Salt and black pepper, to taste
• 1 teaspoon Paprika
• 1 teaspoon Italian seasoning
Preparation:
1. Blend the entire vinaigrette
Ingredients: in a high-speed blender and
pulse into a smooth paste.
2. Set aside for drizzling over the cooked
fish.
3. Rub the fillets with salt, black pepper,
paprika, Italian seasoning, and olive oil.
4. Divide the between two baskets of the
air fryer.
5. Set zone 1 to 16 minutes at 390
degrees F, on AIR FRY mode.
6. Press the MATCH button for zone 2.
7. Once done, serve the fillets with a
drizzle of blended vinaigrette on top.
Serving Suggestion: Serve it with rice
Variation Tip: Use sour cream instead of
cream cheese
Nutritional Information Per Serving:
Calories 1219| Fat 81.8g| Sodium
1906mg | Carbs 64.4g | Fiber 5.5g |
Sugar 0.4g | Protein 52.1g

Fish and Chips

Prep Time: 15 Minutes
Cook Time: 22 Minutes
Serves: 2
Ingredients:
• 1 pound potatoes, cut lengthwise
• 1 cup seasoned flour
• 2 eggs, organic
• ⅓ cup buttermilk
• 2 cups seafood fry mix
• ½ cup bread crumbs
• 2 codfish fillets, 6 ounces each
• Oil spray, for greasing
Preparation:
1. Take a bowl and whisk the eggs in it
along the buttermilk.
2. In a separate bowl, mix the seafood fry
mix and bread crumbs.
3. Take a baking tray and spread some
flour on it.
4. Dip the fillets first in the egg wash,
then in flour, and at the end coat it with
the bread crumbs mixture.
5. Put the fish fillets in thezone 1 basket.
6. Grease the fish fillets with oil spray.
7. Set zone 1 to AIR FRY mode at 400
degrees F for 14 minutes.
8. Put the potatos in zone 2 basket and
lightly grease it with oil spray.
9. Set the zone 2 basket to AIR FRY mode
at 400 degrees F for 22 minutes.
10. Hit the Sync button.
11. Once done, serve and enjoy.
Serving Suggestion: Serve it with
mayonnaise
Variation Tip: Use water instead of
buttermilk
Nutritional Information Per Serving:
Calories 992| Fat 22.3g| Sodium 1406 mg |
Carbs 153.6g | Fiber 10g | Sugar 10g |
Protein 40g

Smoked Salmon

Prep Time: 20 Minutes
Cook Time: 12 Minutes
Serves: 4
Ingredients:
• 2 pounds salmon fillets, smoked
• 6 ounces cream cheese
• 4 tablespoons mayonnaise
• 2 teaspoons chives, fresh
• 1 teaspoon lemon zest
• Salt and freshly ground black pepper, to taste
• 2 tablespoons butter
Preparation:
1. Cut the salmon into very small and uniform bite-size pieces.
2. Mix cream cheese, chives, mayonnaise, black pepper, and lemon zest, in a small mixing bowl.
3. Set it aside for further use.
4. Coat the salmon pieces with salt and butter.
5. Divide the bite-size pieces into both zones of the air fryer.
6. Set it on AIR FRY mode at 400 degrees F for 12 minutes.
7. Select MATCH for zone 2 basket.
8. Once the salmon is done, top it with the cream cheese mixture and serve.
9. Enjoy hot.
Serving Suggestion: Serve it with rice
Variation Tip: Use sour cream instead of cream cheese
Nutritional Information Per Serving:
Calories 557| Fat 15.7g| Sodium 371mg | Carbs 4.8g | Fiber 0g | Sugar 1.1g | Protein 48g

Salmon with Coconut

Prep Time: 10 Minutes
Cook Time: 15 Minutes
Serves: 2
Ingredients:
• Oil spray, for greasing
• 2 salmon fillets, 6 ounces each
• Salt and ground black pepper, to taste
• 1 tablespoon butter, for frying
• 1 tablespoon red curry paste
• 1 cup coconut cream
• 2 tablespoons fresh cilantro, chopped
• 1 cup cauliflower florets
• ½ cup Parmesan cheese, hard
Preparation:
1. Mix salt, black pepper, butter, red curry paste, coconut cream in a bowl and marinate the salmon in it.
2. Oil spray the cauliflower florets and then season with salt and freshly ground black pepper.
3. Place the florets in the zone 1 basket.
4. Layer parchment paper over the zone 2 basket, and then place the salmon fillets on it.
5. Set the zone 2 basket to AIR FRY mode at 15 minutes for 400 degrees F
6. Hit the Sync button to finish it at the same time.
7. Once the time for cooking is over, serve the salmon with cauliflower florets with Parmesan cheese sprinkled on top.
Serving Suggestion: Serve with rice
Variation Tip: Use Mozzarella cheese instead of Parmesan cheese
Nutritional Information Per Serving:
Calories 774 | Fat 59g| Sodium 1223mg | Carbs 12.2g | Fiber 3.9g | Sugar 5.9g | Protein 53.5g

Lemon Pepper Salmon with Asparagus

Prep Time: 20 Minutes
Cook Time: 18 Minutes
Serves: 2

Ingredients:
• 1 cup green asparagus
• 2 tablespoons butter
• 2 fillets salmon, 8 ounces each
• Salt and black pepper, to taste
• 1 teaspoon lemon juice
• ½ teaspoon lemon zest
• Oil spray, for greasing

Preparation:
1. Rinse and trim the asparagus.
2. Rinse and pat dry the salmon fillets.
3. Take a bowl and mix in the lemon juice, lemon zest, salt, and black pepper.
4. Brush the fish fillets with the rub and place them in the zone 1 basket.
5. Place asparagus in the zone 2 basket.
6. Spray the asparagus with oil spray.
7. Set zone 1 to AIR FRY mode for 18 minutes at 390 degrees F.
8. Set the zone 2 to 5 minutes at 390 degrees F on AIR FRY mode.
9. Hit the Sync button to finish at the same time.
10. Once done, serve and enjoy.
Serving Suggestion: Serve it with baked potato
Variation Tip: Use olive oil instead of butter
Nutritional Information Per Serving:
Calories 482| Fat 28g| Sodium 209mg | Carbs 2.8g | Fiber 1.5g | Sugar 1.4g | Protein 56.3g

Keto Baked Salmon with Pesto

Prep Time: 15 Minutes
Cook Time: 18 Minutes
Serves: 2

Ingredients:
• 4 salmon fillets, 2 inches thick
• 2 ounces green pesto
• Salt and black pepper
• ½ tablespoon canola oil, for greasing

Ingredients: for Green Sauce
• 1-½ cups mayonnaise
• 2 tablespoons Greek yogurt
• Salt and black pepper, to taste

Preparation:
1. Rub the salmon with pesto, salt, oil, and black pepper.
2. In a small bowl, whisk together all the green sauce Ingredients:.
3. Divide the fish fillets between both the baskets.
4. Set zone 1 to AIR FRY mode for 18 minutes at 390 degrees F.
5. Select MATCH button for zone 2 basket.
6. Once the cooking is done, serve it with green sauce drizzled on top.
7. Enjoy.
Serving Suggestion: Serve it with mashed cheesy potatoes
Variation Tip: Use butter instead of canal oil
Nutritional Information Per Serving:
Calories 1165 | Fat 80.7g| Sodium 1087mg | Carbs 33.1g | Fiber 0.5g | Sugar 11.5 g | Protein 80.6g

Two-Way Salmon

Prep Time: 10 Minutes
Cook Time: 18 Minutes
Serves: 2
Ingredients:
• 2 salmon fillets, 8 ounces each
• 2 tablespoons Cajun seasoning
• 2 tablespoons Jerk seasoning
• 1 lemon cut in half
• Oil spray, for greasing
Preparation:
1. First, drizzle lemon juice over the salmon and wash them with tap water.
2. Rinse and pat dry the fillets with a paper towel.
3. Rub the fillets with Cajun seasoning and grease with oil spray.
4. Take the second fillet and rub it with Jerk seasoning.
5. Grease the second fillet of with oil spray.
6. Place the salmon fillets in both the baskets.
7. Set the zone 1 basket to 390 degrees F for 16-18 minutes.
8. Select MATCH button for zone 2 basket.
9. Hit the START/STOP button to start cooking.
10. Once the cooking is done, serve the fish hot with mayonnaise.
Serving Suggestion: Serve it with ranch
Variation Tip: None
Nutritional Information Per Serving:
Calories 238| Fat 11.8g| Sodium 488mg | Carbs 9g | Fiber 0g | Sugar 8g | Protein 35g

Shrimp With Lemon and Pepper

Prep Time: 5 minutes
Cook Time: 10 minutes
Serves: 4
Ingredients:
• 1-pound medium raw shrimp, peeled and deveined
• ½ cup olive oil
• 2 tablespoons lemon juice
• 1 teaspoon black pepper
• ½ teaspoon salt
Preparation:
6. Place the shrimp in a Ziploc bag with the olive oil, lemon juice, salt, and pepper. Carefully combine all the Ingredients:.
7. Install a crisper plate in both drawers. Divide the shrimp equally into the two drawers. Insert the drawers into the unit.
8. Select zone 1, then AIR FRY, then set the temperature to 360°F with a 10-minute timer. To match zone 2 settings to zone 1, choose MATCH. To begin, select START/STOP.
9. Remove the shrimp from the drawers after the timer has finished.
Serving Suggestion: Serve the shrimp with pasta.
Variation Tip: You can use lime juice.
Nutritional Information Per Serving:
Calories 322 | Fat 28g | Sodium 909mg | Carbs 2g | Fiber 0g | Sugar 0g | Protein 16g

Fried Tilapia

Prep Time: 5 minutes
Cook Time: 20 minutes
Serves: 4
Ingredients:
• 4 fresh tilapia fillets, approximately 6 ounces each
• 2 teaspoons olive oil
• 2 teaspoons chopped fresh chives
• 2 teaspoons chopped fresh parsley
• 1 teaspoon minced garlic
• Freshly ground pepper, to taste
• Salt to taste
Preparation:
1. Pat the tilapia fillets dry with a paper towel.
2. Stir together the olive oil, chives, parsley, garlic, salt, and pepper in a small bowl.
3. Brush the mixture over the top of the tilapia fillets.
4. Place a crisper plate in each drawer. Add the fillets in a single layer to each drawer. Insert the drawers into the unit.
5. Select zone 1, then AIR FRY, then set the temperature to 360°F with a 20-minute timer. To match zone 2 settings to zone 1, choose MATCH. To begin, select START/STOP.
6. Remove the tilapia fillets from the drawers after the timer has finished.
Serving Suggestion: Serve with a sauce of your choice.
Variation Tip: You can use garlic powder instead of fresh garlic.
Nutritional Information Per Serving:
Calories 140 | Fat 5.7g | Sodium 125mg | Carbs 1.5g | Fiber 0.4g | Sugar 0g | Protein 21.7g

Garlic Butter Salmon

Prep Time: 5 minutes
Cook Time: 10 minutes
Serves: 4
Ingredients:
• 4 (6-ounce) boneless, skin-on salmon fillets (preferably wild-caught)
• 4 tablespoons butter, melted
• 2 teaspoons garlic, minced
• 2 teaspoons fresh Italian parsley, chopped (or ¼ teaspoon dried)
• Salt and pepper to taste
Preparation:
1. Season the fresh salmon with salt and pepper.
2. Mix together the melted butter, garlic, and parsley in a bowl.
3. Baste the salmon fillets with the garlic butter mixture.
4. Place a crisper plate in each drawer. Put 2 fillets in each drawer. Put the drawers inside the unit.
5. Select zone 1, then AIR FRY, then set the temperature to 360°F with a 10-minute timer. To match zone 2 settings to zone 1, choose MATCH. To begin, select START/STOP.
6. Remove the salmon from the drawers after the timer has finished.
Serving Suggestion: Serve with a side salad.
Variation Tip: You can use tuna instead.
Nutritional Information Per Serving:
Calories 338 | Fat 26g | Sodium 309mg | Carbs 1g | Fiber 0g | Sugar 0g | Protein 25g

Spiced Chicken and Vegetables

Prep Time: 22 Minutes
Cook Time: 45 Minutes
Serves: 1

Ingredients:
• 2 large chicken breasts
• 2 teaspoons olive oil
• 1 teaspoon chili powder
• 1 teaspoon Paprika powder
• 1 teaspoon onion powder
• ½ teaspoon garlic powder
• ¼ teaspoon cumin
• Salt and black pepper, to taste

Vegetable Ingredients:
• 2 large potatoes, cubed
• 4 large carrots cut into bite-size pieces
• 1 tablespoon olive oil
• Salt and black pepper, to taste

Preparation:
1. Take chicken breast pieces and rub them with olive oil, salt, pepper, chili powder, onion powder, cumin, garlic powder, and paprika.
2. Season the vegetables with olive oil, salt, and black pepper.
3. Place the chicken breast pieces in the zone 1 basket.
4. Put the vegetables into the zone 2 basket.
5. Set zone 1 to ROAST at 350 degrees F for 45 minutes.
6. For zone 2 set the time for 45 minutes on AIR FRY mode at 350 degrees F.
7. To start cooking hit the Sync button and press START/STOP button.
8. Once the cooking cycle is done, serve, and enjoy.

Serving Suggestion: Serve it with salad or ranch dressing
Variation Tip: Use canola oil instead of olive oil
Nutritional Information Per Serving:
Calories 1510 | Fat 51.3g| Sodium 525mg | Carbs 163g | Fiber 24.7 g | Sugar 21.4g | Protein 102.9

Sesame Ginger Chicken

Prep Time: 10 minutes
Cook Time: 30 minutes
Serves: 4

Ingredients:
• 4 ounces green beans
• 1 tablespoon canola oil
• 1½ pounds boneless, skinless chicken breasts
• ⅓ cup prepared sesame-ginger sauce
• Kosher salt, to taste
• Black pepper, to taste

Preparation:
1. Toss the green beans with a teaspoon of salt and pepper in a medium mixing bowl.
2. Place a crisper plate in each drawer. Place the green beans in the zone 1 drawer and insert it into the unit. Place the chicken breasts in the zone 2 drawer and place it inside the unit.
3. Select zone 1, then AIR FRY, and set the temperature to 390°F with a 10-minute timer. Select zone 2, then AIR FRY, and set the temperature to 390°F with an 18-minute timer. Select SYNC. To begin cooking, press the START/STOP button.
4. Press START/STOP to pause the unit when the zone 2 timer reaches 9 minutes. Remove the chicken from the drawer and toss it in the sesame ginger sauce. To resume cooking, re-insert the drawer into the unit and press START/STOP.
5. When cooking is complete, serve the chicken breasts and green beans straight away.

Serving Suggestion: Serve with steamed or fried rice.
Variation Tip: You can use asparagus instead of green beans.
Nutritional Information Per Serving:
Calories 143 | Fat 7g | Sodium 638mg | Carbs 11.6g | Fiber 1.4g | Sugar 8.5g | Protein 11.1g

Crispy Ranch Nuggets

Prep Time: 15 minutes
Cook Time: 10 minutes
Serves: 4

Ingredients:
- 1 pound chicken tenders, cut into 1½–2-inch pieces
- 1 (1-ounce) sachet dry ranch salad dressing mix
- 2 tablespoons flour
- 1 egg
- 1 cup panko breadcrumbs
- Olive oil cooking spray

Preparation:
1. Toss the chicken with the ranch seasoning in a large mixing bowl. Allow for 5–10 minutes of resting time.
2. Fill a resalable bag halfway with the flour.
3. Crack the egg into a small bowl and lightly beat it.
4. Spread the breadcrumbs onto a dish.
5. Toss the chicken in the bag to coat it. Dip the chicken in the egg mixture lightly, allowing excess to drain off. Roll the chicken pieces in the breadcrumbs, pressing them in, so they stick. Lightly spray with the cooking spray.
6. Install a crisper plate in both drawers. Place half the chicken tenders in the zone 1 drawer and half in the zone 2 one, then insert the drawers into the unit.
7. Select zone 1, select AIR FRY, set temperature to 390°F, and set time to 10 minutes. Select MATCH to match zone 2 settings to zone 1. Press the START/STOP button to begin cooking.
8. When the time reaches 6 minutes, press START/STOP to pause the unit. Remove the drawers and flip the chicken. Re-insert the drawers into the unit and press START/STOP to resume cooking.
9. When cooking is complete, remove the chicken.

Serving Suggestion: Serve with a sauce of your choice.
Variation Tip: You can use almond flour.
Nutritional Information Per Serving:
Calories 244 | Fat 3.6g | Sodium 713mg | Carbs 25.3g | Fiber 0.1g | Sugar 0.1g | Protein 31g

Honey-Cajun Chicken Thighs

Prep Time: 10 minutes
Cook Time: 25 minutes
Serves: 6

Ingredients:
- ½ cup buttermilk
- 1 teaspoon hot sauce
- 1½ pounds skinless, boneless chicken thighs
- ¼ cup all-purpose flour
- ⅓ cup tapioca flour
- 2 ½ teaspoons Cajun seasoning
- ½ teaspoon garlic salt
- ½ teaspoon honey powder
- ¼ teaspoon ground paprika
- ⅛ teaspoon cayenne pepper
- 4 teaspoons honey

Preparation:
1. In a resealable plastic bag, combine the buttermilk and hot sauce. Marinate the chicken thighs in the bag for 30 minutes.
2. Combine the flour, tapioca flour, Cajun spice, garlic salt, honey powder, paprika, and cayenne pepper in a small mixing bowl.
3. Remove the thighs from the buttermilk mixture and dredge them in the flour. Remove any excess flour by shaking it off.
4. Install a crisper plate in both drawers. Place half the chicken thighs in the zone 1 drawer and half in zone 2's, then insert the drawers into the unit.
5. Select zone 1, select AIR FRY, set temperature to 390°F, and set time to 25 minutes. Select MATCH to match zone 2 settings to zone 1. Press the START/STOP button to begin cooking.
6. When the time reaches 11 minutes, press START/STOP to pause the unit. Remove the drawers and flip the chicken. Re-insert the drawers into the unit and press START/STOP to resume cooking.
7. When cooking is complete, remove the chicken and serve.

Serving Suggestion: Serve with a side salad.
Variation Tip: You can use coconut flour.
Nutritional Information Per Serving:
Calories 243 | Fat 11.8g | Sodium 203mg | Carbs 16.1g | Fiber 0.4g | Sugar 5.1g | Protein 19g

Garlic, Buffalo, and Blue Cheese Stuffed Chicken

Prep Time: 15 minutes
Cook Time: 30 minutes
Serves: 2
Ingredients:
• ¼ teaspoon garlic powder
• ¼ teaspoon onion powder
• ¼ teaspoon paprika
• 2 boneless, skinless chicken breasts
• ½ tablespoon canola oil
• 2 ounces softened cream cheese
• ¼ cup shredded cheddar cheese
• ¼ cup blue cheese crumbles
• ¼ cup buffalo sauce
• 1 tablespoon dry ranch seasoning
• 2 tablespoons dried chives
• 1 tablespoon minced garlic
Optional toppings:
• Ranch dressing
• Buffalo sauce
• Fresh parsley
Preparation:
1. Combine the garlic powder, onion powder, and paprika in a small bowl.
2. Drizzle the chicken breasts with oil and season evenly with the garlic powder mixture on a cutting board.
3. Make a deep pocket in the center of each chicken breast, but be cautious not to cut all the way through.
4. Combine the remaining Ingredients: in a medium mixing bowl and stir until thoroughly blended. Fill each chicken breast's pocket with the cream cheese mixture.
5. Place the chicken in both drawers and insert both drawers into the unit. Select zone 1, then BAKE, and set the temperature to 375°F with a 30-minute timer. To match zone 2 and zone 1 settings, select MATCH. To start cooking, use the START/STOP button.
6. Garnish the cooked chicken with ranch dressing, spicy sauce, and parsley on top.
Serving Suggestion: Serve with toppings of your choice.
Variation Tip: You can use red chili flakes.
Nutritional Information Per Serving:
Calories 369 | Fat 23.8g | Sodium 568mg | Carbs 4.3g | Fiber 0.4g | Sugar 0.5g | Protein 34.7g

Thai Chicken Meatballs

Prep Time: 10 minutes
Cook Time: 10 minutes
Serves: 4
Ingredients:
• ½ cup sweet chili sauce
• 2 tablespoons lime juice
• 2 tablespoons ketchup
• 1 teaspoon soy sauce
• 1 large egg, lightly beaten
• ¾ cup panko breadcrumbs
• 1 green onion, finely chopped
• 1 tablespoon minced fresh cilantro
• ½ teaspoon salt
• ½ teaspoon garlic powder
• 1-pound lean ground chicken
Preparation:
1. Combine the chili sauce, lime juice, ketchup, and soy sauce in a small bowl; set aside ½ cup for serving.
2. Combine the egg, breadcrumbs, green onion, cilantro, salt, garlic powder, and the remaining 4 tablespoons chili sauce mixture in a large mixing bowl. Mix in the chicken lightly yet thoroughly. Form into 12 balls.
3. Install a crisper plate in both drawers. Place half the chicken meatballs in the zone 1 drawer and half in zone 2's, then insert the drawers into the unit.
4. Select zone 1, select AIR FRY, set temperature to 390°F, and set time to 10 minutes. Select MATCH to match zone 2 settings to zone 1. Press the START/STOP button to begin cooking.
5. When the time reaches 5 minutes, press START/STOP to pause the unit. Remove the drawers and flip the chicken. Re-insert the drawers into the unit and press START/STOP to resume cooking.
6. When cooking is complete, remove the chicken meatballs and serve hot.
Serving Suggestion: Serve with fried cauliflower rice.
Variation Tip: You can use ground turkey instead.
Nutritional Information Per Serving:
Calories 93 | Fat 3g | Sodium 369mg | Carbs 9g | Fiber 0g | Sugar 6g | Protein 9g

Chicken Cordon Bleu

Prep Time: 10 minutes
Cook Time: 20 minutes
Serves: 4
Ingredients:
• 4 boneless, skinless chicken breast halves (4 ounces each)
• ¼ teaspoon salt
• ¼ teaspoon pepper
• 4 slices deli ham
• 2 slices aged Swiss cheese, halved
• 1 cup panko breadcrumbs
• Cooking spray
For the sauce:
• 1 tablespoon all-purpose flour
• ½ cup 2% milk
• ¼ cup dry white wine
• 3 tablespoons finely shredded Swiss cheese
• $1/8$ teaspoon salt
• Dash pepper
Preparation:
1. Season both sides of the chicken breast halves with salt and pepper. You may need to thin the breasts with a mallet.
2. Place 1 slice of ham and half slice of cheese on top of each chicken breast half.
3. Roll the breast up and use toothpicks to secure it.
4. Sprinkle the breadcrumbs on top and spray lightly with the cooking oil.
5. Insert a crisper plate into each drawer. Divide the chicken between each drawer and insert the drawers into the unit.
6. Select zone 1, select AIR FRY, set temperature to 390°F, and set time to 7 minutes. Select MATCH to match zone 2 settings to zone 1. Press the START/STOP button to begin cooking.
7. When the time reaches 5 minutes, press START/STOP to pause the unit. Remove the drawers and flip the chicken. Re-insert the drawers into the unit and press START/STOP to resume cooking.
8. To make the sauce, mix the flour, wine, and milk together in a small pot until smooth. Bring to a boil over high heat, stirring frequently, for 1–2 minutes, or until the sauce has thickened.
9. Reduce the heat to medium. Add the cheese. Cook and stir for 2–3 minutes, or until the cheese has melted and the sauce has thickened and bubbled. Add salt and pepper to taste. Keep the sauce heated at a low temperature until ready to serve.
Serving Suggestion: Serve the chicken with the sauce drizzled over the top.
Variation Tip: You can use bacon instead of ham.
Nutritional Information Per Serving:
Calories 272 | Fat 8g | Sodium 519mg | Carbs 14g | Fiber 2g | Sugar 1g | Protein 32g

Chicken Leg Piece

Prep Time: 15 Minutes
Cook Time: 25 Minutes
Serves: 1
Ingredients:
• 1 teaspoon onion powder
• 1 teaspoon Paprika powder
• 1 teaspoon garlic powder
• Salt and black pepper, to taste
• 1 tablespoon Italian seasoning
• 1 teaspoon celery seeds
• 2 eggs, whisked
• ⅓ cup buttermilk
• 1 cup cornflour
• 1 pound chicken legs
Preparation:
1. Take a bowl and whisk the eggs along with pepper, salt, and buttermilk and set aside.
2. Mix all the spices in a small separate bowl.
3. Dredge the chicken in the egg wash, then dredge it in the spice seasoning.
4. Coat the chicken legs with oil spray.
5. At the end, dust it with the cornflour.
6. Divide the leg pieces into the two zones.
7. Set zone 1 basket to 400 degrees F for 25 minutes.
8. Select MATCH for zone 2 basket.
9. Let the air fryer do the magic.
10. Once it's done, serve and enjoy.
Serving Suggestion: Serve it with cooked rice
Variation Tip: Use water instead of buttermilk
Nutritional Information Per Serving:
Calories 1511| Fat 52.3g| Sodium 615 mg | Carbs 100g | Fiber 9.2g | Sugar 8.1g | Protein 154.2g

Buttermilk Fried Chicken

Prep Time: 5 minutes (plus 4 hours for marinating)
Cook Time: 30 minutes
Serves: 6

Ingredients:
- 1½ pounds boneless, skinless chicken thighs
- 2 cups buttermilk
- 1 cup all-purpose flour
- 1 tablespoon seasoned salt
- ½ tablespoon ground black pepper
- 1 cup panko breadcrumbs
- Cooking spray

Preparation:
1. Place the chicken thighs in a shallow baking dish. Cover with the buttermilk. Refrigerate for 4 hours or overnight.
2. In a large gallon-sized resealable bag, combine the flour, seasoned salt, and pepper.
3. Remove the chicken from the buttermilk but don't discard the mixture.
4. Add the chicken to the bag and shake well to coat.
5. Dip the thighs in the buttermilk again, then coat in the panko breadcrumbs.
6. Install a crisper plate in each drawer. Place half the chicken thighs in the zone 1 drawer and half in zone 2's, then insert the drawers into the unit.
7. Select zone 1, select AIR FRY, set temperature to 390°F, and set time to 30 minutes. Select MATCH to match zone 2 settings to zone 1. Press the START/STOP button to begin cooking.
8. When the time reaches 15 minutes, press START/STOP to pause the unit. Remove the drawers and flip the chicken. Re-insert the drawers into the unit and press START/STOP to resume cooking.
9. When cooking is complete, remove the chicken.

Serving Suggestion: Serve with fried rice.

Variation Tip: You can use tofu instead of chicken.

Nutritional Information Per Serving:
Calories 335 | Fat 12.8g | Sodium 687mg | Carbs 33.1g | Fiber 0.4g | Sugar 4g | Protein 24.5g

Sweet and Spicy Carrots with Chicken Thighs

Prep Time: 15 Minutes
Cook Time: 35 Minutes
Serves: 2

Ingredients:
Ingredients: for Glaze
- Cooking spray, for greasing
- 2 tablespoons butter, melted
- 1 tablespoon hot honey
- 1 teaspoon orange zest
- 1 teaspoon cardamom
- ½ pound baby carrots
- 1 tablespoon orange juice
- Salt and black pepper, to taste

Other Ingredients:
- ½ pound carrots, baby carrots
- 8 chicken thighs

Preparation:
1. Take a bowl and mix all the glaze Ingredients: in it.
2. Coat the chicken and carrots with the glaze and let them rest for 30 minutes.
3. Place the chicken thighs into zone 1 basket.
4. Put the glazed carrots into the zone 2 basket.
5. Press button 1 for the first basket and set it to ROAST mode at 350 degrees F for 35 minutes.
6. For the second basket hit 2 and set to AIR FRY mode at 390 degrees F for 8-10 minutes.
7. Press Sync button so both finish at the same time.
8. Once the cooking cycle is complete, take out the carrots and chicken and serve it hot.

Serving Suggestion: Serve with salad
Variation Tip: Use lime juice instead of orange juice

Nutritional Information Per Serving:
Calories 1312| Fat 55.4g| Sodium 757mg | Carbs 23.3g | Fiber 6.7g | Sugar 12g | Protein 171g

Chicken Wings

Prep Time: 10 minutes
Cook Time: 45 minutes
Serves: 4
Ingredients:
• 2 pounds chicken wings
• Kosher salt
• Freshly ground black pepper
• Non-stick cooking spray
• ¼ cup hot sauce (such as Frank's)
• 4 tablespoons melted butter
• 1 teaspoon Worcestershire sauce
• ½ teaspoon garlic powder
Preparation:
1. Season the wings with salt and pepper. Spray the inside of the drawers with non-stick spray.
2. Place a crisper plate in each drawer. Put half of the chicken wings in the zone 1 drawer and half in the zone 2 drawer, then insert the drawers into the unit.
3. Select zone 1, select AIR FRY, set temperature to 400°F, and set time to 45 minutes. Select MATCH to match zone 2 settings to zone 1. Press the START/STOP button to begin cooking.
4. When the time reaches 22 minutes, press START/STOP to pause the cooking. Remove the drawers and flip the chicken. Re-insert the drawers into the unit and press START/STOP to resume cooking.
5. When cooking is complete, remove the chicken wings.
6. Meanwhile, combine the hot sauce, butter, Worcestershire sauce, and garlic powder in a large bowl. Add the cooked wings to the mixture and toss gently to coat. Serve hot.
Serving Suggestion: Serve with a side salad.
Variation Tip: You can use fresh garlic.
Nutritional Information Per Serving:
Calories 538 | Fat 28.5g | Sodium 710mg | Carbs 0.8g | Fiber 0.1g | Sugar 0.5g | Protein 65.9g

Whole Chicken

Prep Time: 10 minutes
Cook Time: 20 minutes
Serves: 8
Ingredients:
• 1 whole chicken (about 2.8 pounds), cut in half
• 4 tablespoons olive oil
• 2 teaspoons paprika
• 1 teaspoon garlic powder
• 1 teaspoon onion powder
• Salt and pepper, to taste
Preparation:
1. Mix the olive oil, paprika, garlic powder, and onion powder together in a bowl.
2. Place the chicken halves, breast side up, on a plate. Spread a teaspoon or two of the oil mix all over the halves using either your hands or a brush. Season with salt and pepper.
3. Flip the chicken halves over and repeat on the other side. You'll want to reserve a little of the oil mix for later, but other than that, use it liberally.
4. Install a crisper plate in both drawers. Place one half of the chicken in the zone 1 drawer and the other half in the zone 2 drawer, then insert the drawers into the unit.
5. Select zone 1, select AIR FRY, set temperature to 390°F, and set time to 20 minutes. Select MATCH to match zone 2 settings to zone 1. Press the START/STOP button to begin cooking.
6. When cooking is done, check the internal temperature of the chicken. It should read 165°F. If the chicken isn't done, add more cooking time.
Serving Suggestion: Serve with veggies of your choice.
Variation Tip: Use red chili flakes for some kick.
Nutritional Information Per Serving:
Calories 131 | Fat 8g | Sodium 51mg | Carbs 0g | Fiber 0g | Sugar 0g | Protein 14g

Chicken Ranch Wraps

Prep Time: 5 minutes
Cook Time: 22 minutes
Serves: 4

Ingredients:
• 1½ ounces breaded chicken breast tenders
• 4 (12-inch) whole-wheat tortilla wraps
• 2 heads romaine lettuce, chopped
• ½ cup shredded mozzarella cheese
• 4 tablespoons ranch dressing

Preparation:
1. Place a crisper plate in each drawer. Place half of the chicken tenders in one drawer and half in the other. Insert the drawers into the unit.
2. Select zone 1, then AIR FRY, and set the temperature to 390°F with a 22-minute timer. To match zone 2 settings to zone 1, choose MATCH. To begin cooking, press the START/STOP button.
3. To pause the unit, press START/STOP when the timer reaches 11 minutes. Remove the drawers from the unit and flip the tenders over. To resume cooking, re-insert the drawers into the device and press START/STOP.
4. Remove the chicken from the drawers when they're done cooking and chop them up.
5. Divide the chopped chicken between warmed-up wraps. Top with some lettuce, cheese, and ranch dressing. Wrap and serve.

Serving Suggestion: You can add extra toppings of your choice.

Variation Tip: Use any cheese you prefer.

Nutritional Information Per Serving:
Calories 212 | Fat 7.8g | Sodium 567mg | Carbs 9.1g | Fiber 34.4g | Sugar 9.7g | Protein 10.6g

Buffalo Chicken

Prep Time: 20 minutes
Cook Time: 22 minutes
Serves: 4

Ingredients:
• ½ cup plain fat-free Greek yogurt
• ¼ cup egg substitute
• 1 tablespoon plus 1 teaspoon hot sauce
• 1 cup panko breadcrumbs
• 1 tablespoon sweet paprika
• 1 tablespoon garlic pepper seasoning
• 1 tablespoon cayenne pepper
• 1-pound skinless, boneless chicken breasts, cut into 1-inch strips

Preparation:
1. Combine the Greek yogurt, egg substitute, and hot sauce in a mixing bowl.
2. In a separate bowl, combine the panko breadcrumbs, paprika, garlic powder, and cayenne pepper.
3. Dip the chicken strips in the yogurt mixture, then coat them in the breadcrumb mixture.
4. Install a crisper plate in both drawers. Place the chicken strips into the drawers and then insert the drawers into the unit.
5. Select zone 1, select AIR FRY, set temperature to 390°F, and set time to 22 minutes. Select MATCH to match zone 2 settings to zone 1. Press the START/STOP button to begin cooking.
6. When cooking is complete, serve immediately.

Serving Suggestion: Serve with a dipping sauce of your choice.

Variation Tip: You can use regular breadcrumbs instead of panko.

Nutritional Information Per Serving:
Calories 234 | Fat 15.8g | Sodium 696mg | Carbs 22.1g | Fiber 1.1g | Sugar 1.7g | Protein 31.2g

Chicken Parmesan

Prep Time: 10 minutes
Cook Time: 20 minutes
Serves: 4
Ingredients:
• 2 large eggs
• ½ cup seasoned breadcrumbs
• ⅓ cup grated parmesan cheese
• ¼ teaspoon pepper
• 4 boneless, skinless chicken breast halves (6 ounces each)
• 1 cup pasta sauce
• 1 cup shredded mozzarella cheese
• Chopped fresh basil (optional)
Preparation:
1. Lightly beat the eggs in a small bowl.
2. Combine the breadcrumbs, parmesan cheese, and pepper in a shallow bowl.
3. After dipping the chicken in the egg, coat it in the crumb mixture.
4. Install a crisper plate in both drawers. Place half the chicken breasts in the zone 1 drawer and half in zone 2's, then insert the drawers into the unit.
5. Select zone 1, select AIR FRY, set temperature to 390°F, and set time to 20 minutes. Select MATCH to match zone 2 settings to zone 1. Press the START/STOP button to begin cooking.
6. When the time reaches 10 minutes, press START/STOP to pause the unit. Remove the drawers and flip the chicken. Re-insert the drawers into the unit and press START/STOP to resume cooking.
7. When cooking is complete, remove the chicken.
Serving Suggestion: Serve with pasta and garnish with fresh basil.
Variation Tip: You can use panko breadcrumbs if you prefer.
Nutritional Information Per Serving:
Calories 293 | Fat 15.8g | Sodium 203mg | Carbs 11.1g | Fiber 2.4g | Sugar 8.7g | Protein 29g

Almond Chicken

Prep Time: 10 minutes
Cook Time: 25 minutes
Serves: 4
Ingredients:
• 2 large eggs
• ½ cup buttermilk
• 2 teaspoons garlic salt
• 1 teaspoon pepper
• 2 cups slivered almonds, finely chopped
• 4 boneless, skinless chicken breast halves (6 ounces each)
Preparation:
1. Whisk together the egg, buttermilk, garlic salt, and pepper in a small bowl.
2. In another small bowl, place the almonds.
3. Dip the chicken in the egg mixture, then roll it in the almonds, patting it down to help the coating stick.
4. Install a crisper plate in both drawers. Place half the chicken breasts in the zone 1 drawer and half in zone 2's, then insert the drawers into the unit.
5. Select zone 1, select AIR FRY, set temperature to 390°F, and set time to 22 minutes. Select MATCH to match zone 2 settings to zone 1. Press the START/STOP button to begin cooking.
6. When the time reaches 11 minutes, press START/STOP to pause the unit. Remove the drawers and flip the chicken. Re-insert the drawers into the unit and press START/STOP to resume cooking.
7. When cooking is complete, remove the chicken.
Serving Suggestion: Serve with a sauce of your choice.
Variation Tip: You can use walnuts instead.
Nutritional Information Per Serving:
Calories 353 | Fat 18g | Sodium 230mg | Carbs 6g | Fiber 2g | Sugar 3g | Protein 41g

Chicken Thighs with Brussels sprouts

Prep Time: 20 Minutes
Cook Time: 30 Minutes
Serves: 2
Ingredients:
• 2 tablespoons honey
• 4 tablespoons Dijon mustard
• Salt and black pepper, to tat
• 4 tablespoons olive oil
• 1-½ cups Brussels sprouts
• 8 chicken thighs, skinless
Preparation:
1. Take a bowl and add chicken thighs to it.
2. Add honey, Dijon mustard, salt, pepper, and 2 tablespoons of olive oil to the thighs.
3. Coat the chicken well and marinate it for 1 hour.
4. Season the Brussels sprouts with salt and black pepper along with the remaining olive oil.
5. Place the chicken in the zone 1 basket.
6. Put the Brussels sprouts into the zone 2 basket.
7. Select ROAST mode for chicken and set time to 30 minutes at 390 degrees F.
8. Select AIR FRY mode for Brussels sprouts and set the timer to 20 minutes at 400 degrees F.
9. Once done, serve and enjoy.
Serving Suggestion: Serve it with BBQ sauce
Variation Tip: You can use canola oil instead of olive oil
Nutritional Information Per Serving:
Calories 1454 | Fat 72.2g| Sodium 869mg | Carbs 23g | Fiber 2.7g | Sugar 19g | Protein 172g

Cornish Hen with Baked Potatoes

Prep Time: 20 Minutes
Cook Time: 45 Minutes
Serves: 2
Ingredients:
• Salt, to taste
• 1 large potato
• 1 tablespoon avocado oil
• 1.5 pounds Cornish hen, skinless and whole
• 2-3 teaspoons poultry seasoning, dry rub
Preparation:
1. Pierce the large potato with a fork.
2. Rub the potato with avocado oil and salt.
3. Place the potato in the first basket.
4. Coat the Cornish hen thoroughly with poultry seasoning (dry rub) and salt.
5. Place the hen in zone 2 basket.
6. Set zone 1 to AIR FRY mode at 350 degrees F for 45 minutes.
7. For zone 2 press the MATCH button.
8. Once the cooking cycle is complete, turn off the air fryer and take out the potatoes and Cornish hen from both air fryer baskets.
9. Serve hot and enjoy.
Serving Suggestion: Serve it with coleslaw
Variation Tip: You can use olive oil or canola oil instead of avocado oil
Nutritional Information Per Serving:
Calories 612 | Fat 14.3g| Sodium 304mg | Carbs 33.4 g | Fiber 4.5g | Sugar 1.5g | Protein 83.2g

Spicy Chicken

Prep Time: 12 Minutes
Cook Time: 35-40 Minutes
Serves: 4
Ingredients:
• 4 chicken thighs
• 2 cups buttermilk
• 4 chicken legs
• 2 cups flour
• Salt and black pepper, to taste
• 2 tablespoons garlic powder
• ½ teaspoon onion powder
• 1 teaspoon poultry seasoning
• 1 teaspoon cumin
• 2 tablespoons Paprika
• 1 tablespoon olive oil
Preparation:
1. Take a bowl and add the buttermilk to it.
2. Soak the chicken thighs and chicken legs in the buttermilk for 2 hours.
3. Mix the flour, all the seasonings, and olive oil in a small bowl.
4. Take out the chicken pieces from the buttermilk mixture and then dredge them into the flour mixture.
5. Repeat the step for all the pieces and then arrange them in both the air fryer baskets.
6. Set the timer for both the baskets to ROAST mode for 35-40 minutes at 350 degrees F.
7. Once the cooking cycle is complete take them out and serve hot.
Serving Suggestion: Serve the chicken with garlic dipping sauce
Variation Tip: Use canola oil instead of olive oil
Nutritional Information Per Serving:
Calories 624| Fat 17.6g| Sodium 300mg | Carbs 60g | Fiber 3.5g | Sugar 7.7g | Protein 54.2g

Chicken Tenders and Curly Fries

Prep Time: 5 minutes
Cook Time: 35 minutes
Serves: 4
Ingredients:
• 1-pound frozen chicken tenders
• 1-pound frozen curly French fries
• Dipping sauces of your choice
Preparation:
1. Place a crisper plate in each drawer. In the zone 1 drawer, place the chicken tenders, then place the drawer into the unit.
2. Fill the zone 2 drawer with the curly French fries, then place the drawer in the unit.
3. Select zone 1, then AIR FRY, and set the temperature to 390°F with a 22-minute timer. Select zone 2, then AIR FRY, and set the temperature to 400°F with a 30-minute timer. Select SYNC. To begin cooking, press the START/STOP button.
4. Press START/STOP to pause the device when the zone 1 and 2 times reach 8 minutes. Shake the drawers for 10 seconds after removing them from the unit. To resume cooking, re-insert the drawers into the unit and press START/STOP.
5. Enjoy!
Serving Suggestion: Serve with dipping sauces of your choice.
Variation Tip: You can use turkey tenders instead of chicken.
Nutritional Information Per Serving:
Calories 500 | Fat 19.8g | Sodium 680mg | Carbs 50.1g | Fiber 4.1g | Sugar 0g | Protein 27.9g

Yummy Chicken Breasts

Prep Time: 15 Minutes
Cook Time: 25 Minutes
Serves: 2
Ingredients:
• 4 large chicken breasts, 6 ounces each
• 2 tablespoons oil bay seasoning
• 1 tablespoon Montreal chicken seasoning
• 1 teaspoon thyme
• ½ teaspoon Paprika
• Salt, to taste
• Oil spray, for greasing
Preparation:
1. Season the chicken breast pieces with the listed seasoning and let them rest for 40 minutes.
2. Grease both sides of the chicken breast pieces with oil spray.
3. Divide the pieces between both baskets.
4. Set zone 1 to AIR FRY mode at 400 degrees F for 15 minutes.
5. Select the MATCH button for zone 2 basket.
6. Press START/STOP and take out the baskets and flip the chicken breast pieces.
7. Select the zones to 400 degrees F for 10 more minutes using the MATCH button.
8. Once it's done serve and enjoy.
Serving Suggestion: Serve with baked potato
Variation Tip: None
Nutritional Information Per Serving:
Calories 711| Fat 27.7g| Sodium 895mg | Carbs 1.6g | Fiber 0.4g | Sugar 0.1g | Protein 106.3g

Glazed Thighs with French Fries

Prep Time: 22 Minutes
Cook Time: 35 Minutes
Serves: 3
Ingredients:
• 2 tablespoons soy sauce
• Salt, to taste
• 1 teaspoon Worcestershire sauce
• 2 teaspoons brown sugar
• 1 teaspoon ginger paste
• 1 teaspoon garlic paste
• 6 boneless chicken thighs
• 1 pound hand-cut potato fries
• 2 tablespoons of canola oil
Preparation:
1. Coat the French fries well with canola oil and season with salt.
2. In a small bowl, combine the soy sauce, Worcestershire sauce, brown sugar, ginger, and garlic.
3. Place the chicken in this marinade and let it sit for 40 minutes.
4. Put the chicken thighs into the zone 1 basket and fries into the zone 2 basket.
5. Press button 1 for the first basket, and set it to ROAST mode at 350 degrees F for 35 minutes.
6. For the second basket hit 2 and set time to 30 minutes at 360 degrees F on AIR FRY mode.
7. Once the cooking cycle is complete, take out the fries and chicken. Serve it hot.
Serving Suggestion: Serve with ketchup
Variation Tip: You can use honey instead of brown sugar
Nutritional Information Per Serving:
Calories 858| Fat 39g | Sodium 1509mg | Carbs 45.6g | Fiber 4.4g | Sugar 3g | Protein 90g

Chicken Breast Strips

Prep Time: 10 Minutes
Cook Time: 22 Minutes
Serves: 2

Ingredients:
• 2 large organic eggs
• 1-ounce buttermilk
• 1 cup cornmeal
• ¼ cup all-purpose flour
• Salt and black pepper, to taste
• 1 pound chicken breasts, cut into strips
• 2 tablespoons oil bay seasoning
• Oil spray, for greasing

Preparation:
1. Take a medium bowl and whisk the eggs with buttermilk.
2. In a separate large bowl, mix flour, cornmeal, salt, black pepper, and oil bay seasoning.
3. First, dip the chicken breast strip in egg wash and then dredge into the flour mixture.
4. Grease the air fryer baskets and divide the chicken strips into them.
5. Set the zone 1 basket to AIR FRY mode at 400 degrees F for 22 minutes.
6. Select the MATCH button for zone 2.
7. Hit the START/STOP button to let the cooking start.
8. Once the cooking cycle is done, serve.

Serving Suggestion: Serve it with roasted vegetables
Variation Tip: None
Nutritional Information Per Serving:
Calories 788| Fat 25g| Sodium 835 mg | Carbs60g | Fiber 4.9g| Sugar 1.5g | Protein 79g

Chapter 6 Beef, Pork, and Lamb Recipes

Breaded Pork Chops

Prep Time: 10 minutes
Cook Time: 10 minutes
Serves: 4
Ingredients:
• 4 boneless, center-cut pork chops, 1-inch thick
• 1 teaspoon Cajun seasoning
• 1½ cups cheese and garlic-flavored croutons
• 2 eggs
• Cooking spray
Preparation:
1. Season both sides of the pork chops with the Cajun seasoning on a platter.
2. In a small food processor, pulse the croutons until finely chopped; transfer to a shallow plate.
3. In a separate shallow bowl, lightly beat the eggs.
4. Dip the pork chops in the egg, allowing any excess to drip off. Then place the chops in the crouton crumbs. Coat the chops in cooking spray.
5. Install a crisper plate in both drawers. Place half the pork chops in the zone 1 drawer and half in zone 2's, then insert the drawers into the unit.
6. Select zone 1, select ROAST, set temperature to 390°F, and set time to 10 minutes. Select MATCH to match zone 2 settings to zone 1. Press the START/STOP button to begin cooking.
7. When the time reaches 6 minutes, press START/STOP to pause the unit. Remove the drawers and flip the chops. Reinsert the drawers into the unit and press START/STOP to resume cooking.
8. When cooking is complete, serve and enjoy!
Serving Suggestion: Serve with a sauce of your choice.
Variation Tip: You can use beef chops instead.
Nutritional Information Per Serving:
Calories 394 | Fat 18.1g | Sodium 428mg | Carbs 10g | Fiber 0.8g | Sugar 0.9g | Protein 44.7g

Beef Ribs II

Prep Time: 20 Minutes
Cook Time: 1 Hour
Serves: 2
Ingredients:
for Marinade:
• ¼ cup olive oil
• 4 garlic cloves, minced
• ½ cup white wine vinegar
• ¼ cup soy sauce, reduced-sodium
• ¼ cup Worcestershire sauce
• 1 lemon juice
• Salt and black pepper, to taste
• 2 tablespoons Italian seasoning
• 1 teaspoon smoked Paprika
• 2 tablespoons mustard
• ½ cup maple syrup
Meat Ingredients:
• Oil spray, for greasing
• 8 beef ribs lean
Preparation:
1. Take a large bowl and add all the marinade Ingredients: and mix well then place into a zip lock bag along with the ribs. Let it sit for 4 hours.
2. Grease the air fryer baskets and divide the ribs into them.
3. Set zone 1 to AIR FRY mode at 220 degrees F for 30 minutes.
4. Select MATCH button for zone 2.
5. After the time is up, select START/STOP and take out the baskets.
6. Flip the ribs and cook for 30 more minutes at 250 degrees F.
7. Once done, serve the juicy and tender ribs.
8. Enjoy.
Serving Suggestion: Serve it with mac and cheese
Variation Tip: Use garlic-infused oil instead of garlic cloves
Nutritional Information Per Serving:
Calories 1927| Fat 116g| Sodium 1394mg | Carbs 35.2g | Fiber 1.3g| Sugar29 g | Protein 172.3g

Beef & Broccoli

Prep Time: 12 Minutes
Cook Time: 12 Minutes
Serves: 4
Ingredients:
• 12 ounces Teriyaki sauce, divided
• ½ tablespoon garlic powder
• ¼ cup soy sauce
• 1 pound raw sirloin steak, thinly sliced
• 2 cups broccoli, cut into florets
• 2 teaspoons olive oil
• Salt and black pepper, to taste
Preparation:
1. Mix the Teriyaki sauce, salt, garlic powder, black pepper, soy sauce, and olive oil in a zip-lock bag.
2. Add the beef and let it marinate for 2 hours.
3. Drain the beef from the marinade.
4. Toss the broccoli with oil, teriyaki sauce, and salt and black pepper and place in the zone 1 basket.
5. Place the beef in both baskets and set it to SYNC button.
6. Hit START/STOP button and let the cooking cycle complete.
7. Once it's done, take out the beef and broccoli and serve with the leftover Teriyaki sauce and cooked rice.
Serving Suggestion: Serve it with mashed potatoes
Variation Tip: Use canola oil instead of olive oil
Nutritional Information Per Serving:
Calories 344| Fat 10g| Sodium 4285mg | Carbs 18.2 g | Fiber 1.5g| Sugar 13.3g | Protein 42g

Beef Ribs I

Prep Time: 10 Minutes
Cook Time: 15 Minutes
Serves: 2
Ingredients:
• 4 tablespoons BBQ spice rub
• 1 tablespoon kosher salt and black pepper
• 3 tablespoons brown sugar
• 2 pounds of beef ribs cut in thirds
• 1 cup BBQ sauce
• Oil spray
Preparation:
1. In a small bowl, add salt, pepper, brown sugar, and BBQ spice rub.

2. Grease the ribs with oil spray from both sides and then rub it with BBQ the spice.
3. Divide the ribs into both baskets and set zone 1to AIR FRY mode at 375 degrees F for 15 minutes.
4. Press MATCH for zone 2.
5. Hit START/STOP button and let the air fryer cook the ribs.
6. Once done, serve with a coating BBQ sauce.
Serving Suggestion: Serve it with salad and baked potato
Variation Tip: Use sea salt instead of kosher salt
Nutritional Information Per Serving:
Calories 1081 | Fat 28.6 g| Sodium 1701mg | Carbs 58g | Fiber 0.8g| Sugar 45.7g | Protein 138 g

Spicy Lamb Chops

Prep Time: 15 Minutes
Cook Time: 15 Minutes
Serves: 4
Ingredients:
• 12 lamb chops, bone-in
• Salt and black pepper, to taste
• ½ teaspoon lemon zest
• 1 tablespoon lemon juice
• 1 teaspoon paprika
• 1 teaspoon garlic powder
• ½ teaspoon Italian seasoning
• ¼ teaspoon onion powder
Preparation:
1. Add the lamb chops to the bowl and sprinkle with salt, garlic powder, Italian seasoning, onion powder, black pepper, lemon zest, lemon juice, and paprika.
2. Rub the chops well, and divide them between both the baskets of the air fryer.
3. Set zone 1 basket to 400 degrees F, for 15 minutes on AIR FRY mode.
4. Select MATCH for zone 2 basket.
5. After 10 minutes, take out the baskets and flip the chops. Cook for the remaining minutes, and then serve.
Serving Suggestion: Serve it over rice
Variation Tip: None
Nutritional Information Per Serving:
Calories 787| Fat 45.3g| Sodium 1mg | Carbs 16.1g | Fiber 0.3g | Sugar 0.4g | Protein 75.3g

Steak in Air Fry

Prep Time: 15 Minutes
Cook Time: 20 Minutes
Serves: 1
Ingredients:
• 2 teaspoons canola oil
• 1 tablespoon Montreal Steak seasoning
• 1 pound beef steak
Preparation:
1. Season the steak on both sides with canola oil and then rub a generous amount of steak seasoning all over.
2. Put the steak in the air fryer basket in zone 1and set it to MAX CRISP at 450 degrees F for 20-22 minutes.
3. After 7 minutes, hit pause, take out the basket to flip the steak and cover it with foil on top for the remaining 14 minutes.
4. Once done, serve the medium-rare steak after it has rested for 10 minutes.
5. Serve by cutting into slices.
6. Enjoy.
Serving Suggestion: Serve it with mashed potatoes
Variation Tip: Use vegetable oil instead of canola oil
Nutritional Information Per Serving:
Calories 935| Fat 37.2g| Sodium 1419mg | Carbs 0g | Fiber 0g| Sugar 0g | Protein 137.5 g

Juicy Pork Chops

Prep Time: 5 minutes
Cook Time: 15 minutes
Serves: 4
Ingredients:
• 4 thick-cut pork chops
• Salt and pepper, to taste
• 2 tablespoons brown sugar
• 1 teaspoon chili powder
• ½ teaspoon paprika
• 1 teaspoon Italian seasoning
• 1 teaspoon garlic powder
Preparation:
1. Salt and pepper the pork chops.
2. Add the brown sugar, chili powder, paprika, Italian seasoning, and garlic powder to a small bowl. Combine well. Rub the mixture on the pork chops.
3. Install a crisper plate in both drawers. Place half the pork chops in the zone 1 drawer and half in zone 2's. Insert the drawers into the unit.
4. Select zone 1, select AIR FRY, set temperature to 400°F, and set time to 15 minutes. Select MATCH to match zone 2 settings to zone 1. Press the START/STOP button to begin cooking.
5. When the time reaches 11 minutes, press START/STOP to pause the unit. Remove the drawers and flip the chops. Re-insert the drawers into the unit and press START/STOP to resume cooking.
6. Serve and enjoy!
Serving Suggestion: Serve with a sauce of your choice.
Variation Tip: You can use beef chops instead.
Nutritional Information Per Serving:
Calories 265 | Fat 10g | Sodium 86mg | Carbs 14g | Fiber 4.1g | Sugar 0g | Protein 29g

Pork Chops

Prep Time: 10 Minutes
Cook Time: 17 Minutes
Serves: 2
Ingredients:
• 1 tablespoon rosemary, chopped
• Salt and black pepper, to taste
• 2 garlic cloves
• 1-inch ginger
• 2 tablespoons olive oil
• 8 pork chops
Preparation:
1. Take a blender and pulse rosemary, salt, pepper, garlic cloves, ginger, and olive oil.
2. Rub this marinade over the pork chops and let it rest for 1 hour.
3. Divide the chops into both the baskets. Set zone 1 to AIR FRY mode for 17 minutes.
4. Select the MATCH button for zone 2.
5. Once done, take out and serve hot.
Serving Suggestion: Serve with salad
Variation Tip: Use canola oil instead of olive oil
Nutritional Information Per Serving:
Calories 1154| Fat 93.8g| Sodium 225mg | Carbs 2.1g | Fiber0.8 g| Sugar 0g | Protein 72.2g

Lamb Chops With Dijon Garlic

Prep Time: 10 minutes (plus 30 minutes for marinating)
Cook Time: 22 minutes
Serves: 4
Ingredients:
• 2 teaspoons Dijon mustard
• 2 teaspoons olive oil
• 1 teaspoon soy sauce
• 1 teaspoon garlic, minced
• 1 teaspoon cumin powder
• 1 teaspoon cayenne pepper
• 1 teaspoon Italian spice blend (optional)
• ¼ teaspoon salt
• 8 lamb chops
Preparation:
1. Combine the Dijon mustard, olive oil, soy sauce, garlic, cumin powder, cayenne pepper, Italian spice blend (optional), and salt in a medium mixing bowl.
2. Put the marinade in a large Ziploc bag. Add the lamb chops. Seal the bag tightly after pressing out the air. Coat the lamb in the marinade by shaking the bag and pressing the chops into the mixture. Place in the fridge for at least 30 minutes, or up to overnight, to marinate.
3. Install a crisper plate in both drawers. Place half the lamb chops in the zone 1 drawer and half in zone 2's, then insert the drawers into the unit.
4. Select zone 1, select AIR FRY, set temperature to 390°F, and set time to 22 minutes. Select MATCH to match zone 2 settings to zone 1. Press the START/STOP button to begin cooking.
5. When the time reaches 11 minutes, press START/STOP to pause the unit. Remove the drawers and flip the lamb chops. Re-insert the drawers into the unit and press START/STOP to resume cooking.
6. Serve and enjoy!
Serving Suggestion: Serve with grilled veggies.
Variation Tip: You can use pork chops.
Nutritional Information Per Serving:
Calories 343 | Fat 15.1g | Sodium 380mg | Carbs 0.9 g | Fiber 0.3g | Sugar 0.1g | Protein 48.9g

Paprika Pork Chops

Prep Time: 10 minutes
Cook Time: 12 minutes
Serves: 4
Ingredients:
• 4 bone-in pork chops (6–8 ounces each)
• 1½ tablespoons brown sugar
• 1¼ teaspoons kosher salt
• 1 teaspoon dried Italian seasoning
• 1 teaspoon smoked paprika
• ¼ teaspoon garlic powder
• ¼ teaspoon onion powder
• ¼ teaspoon black pepper
• 1 teaspoon sweet paprika
• 3 tablespoons butter, melted
• 2 tablespoons chopped fresh parsley
• Cooking spray
Preparation:
1. In a small mixing bowl, combine the brown sugar, salt, Italian seasoning, smoked paprika, garlic powder, onion powder, black pepper, and sweet paprika. Mix thoroughly.
2. Brush the pork chops on both sides with the melted butter.
3. Rub the spice mixture all over the meat on both sides.
4. Install a crisper plate in both drawers. Place half the chops in the zone 1 drawer and half in zone 2's, then insert the drawers into the unit.
5. Select zone 1, select AIR FRY, set temperature to 390°F, and set time to 12 minutes. Select MATCH to match zone 2 settings to zone 1. Press the START/STOP button to begin cooking.
6. When the time reaches 10 minutes, press START/STOP to pause the unit. Remove the drawers and flip the chops. Re-insert the drawers into the unit and press START/STOP to resume cooking.
7. Serve and enjoy!
Serving Suggestion: Serve with a side salad.
Variation Tip: You can use lamb chops instead.
Nutritional Information Per Serving:
Calories 338 | Fat 21.2g | Sodium 1503mg | Carbs 5.1g | Fiber 0.3g | Sugar 4.6g | Protein 29.3g

Jerk-Rubbed Pork Loin With Carrots and Sage

Prep Time: 10 minutes
Cook Time: 35 minutes
Serves: 4

Ingredients:
- 1½ pounds pork loin
- 3 teaspoons canola oil, divided
- 2 tablespoons jerk seasoning
- 1-pound carrots, peeled, cut into 1-inch pieces
- 1 tablespoon honey
- ½ teaspoon kosher salt
- ½ teaspoon chopped fresh sage

Preparation:
1. Place the pork loin in a pan or a dish with a high wall. Using a paper towel, pat the meat dry.
2. Rub 2 teaspoons of canola oil evenly over the pork with your hands. Then spread the jerk seasoning evenly over it with your hands.
3. Allow the pork loin to marinate for at least 10 minutes or up to 8 hours in the refrigerator after wrapping it in plastic wrap or sealing it in a plastic bag.
4. Toss the carrots with the remaining canola oil and ½ teaspoon of salt in a medium mixing bowl.
5. Place a crisper plate in each of the drawers. Put the marinated pork loin in the zone 1 drawer and place it in the unit. Place the carrots in the zone 2 drawer and place the drawer in the unit.
6. Select zone 1 and select AIR FRY. Set the temperature to 390°F and the time setting to 25 minutes. Select zone 2 and select AIR FRY. Set the temperature to 390°F and the time setting to 16 minutes. Select SYNC. Press START/STOP to begin cooking.
7. Check the pork loin for doneness after the zones have finished cooking. When the internal temperature of the loin hits 145°F on an instant-read thermometer, the pork is ready.
8. Allow the pork loin to rest for at least 5 minutes on a plate or cutting board.
9. Combine the carrots and sage in a mixing bowl.
10. When the pork loin has rested, slice it into the desired thickness of slices and serve with the carrots.

Serving Suggestion: Serve with a side salad.
Variation Tip: You can use beef instead.
Nutritional Information Per Serving: Calories 500 | Fat 19.8g | Sodium 680mg | Carbs 50.1g | Fiber 4.1g | Sugar 0g | Protein 27.9g

Glazed Steak Recipe

Prep Time: 15 Minutes
Cook Time: 25 Minutes
Serves: 2

Ingredients:
- 1 pound beef steaks
- ½ cup, soy sauce
- Salt and black pepper, to taste
- 1 tablespoon vegetable oil
- 1 teaspoon grated ginger
- 4 cloves garlic, minced
- ¼ cup brown sugar

Preparation:
1. Whisk together soy sauce, salt, pepper, vegetable oil, garlic, brown sugar, and ginger in a bowl.
2. Once a paste is made from the mixture, rub the steak with it and let it sit for 30 minutes.
3. Add the steak to the air fryer basket and set it to MAX CRISP mode at 400 degrees F for 18-22 minutes.
4. After 10 minutes, hit START/STOP and take it out to flip and return to the air fryer.
5. Once the time is complete, take out the steak and let it rest. Serve by cutting into slices.
6. Enjoy.

Serving Suggestion: Serve it with mashed potatoes
Variation Tip: Use canola oil instead of vegetable oil
Nutritional Information Per Serving: Calories 563| Fat 21 g| Sodium 156mg | Carbs 20.6g | Fiber 0.3 g| Sugar 17.8 g | Protein 69.4 g

Meatloaf

Prep Time: 10 minutes
Cook Time: 25 minutes
Serves: 6
Ingredients:
For the meatloaf:
• 2 pounds ground beef
• 2 eggs, beaten
• 2 cups old-fashioned oats, regular or gluten-free
• ½ cup evaporated milk
• ½ cup chopped onion
• ½ teaspoon garlic salt
For the sauce:
• 1 cup ketchup
• ¾ cup brown sugar, packed
• ¼ cup chopped onion
• ½ teaspoon liquid smoke
• ¼ teaspoon garlic powder
• Olive oil cooking spray
Preparation:
1. In a large bowl, combine all the meatloaf Ingredients:.
2. Spray 2 sheets of foil with olive oil cooking spray.
3. Form the meatloaf mixture into a loaf shape, cut in half, and place each half on one piece of foil.
4. Roll the foil up a bit on the sides. Allow it to be slightly open.
5. Put all the sauce Ingredients: in a saucepan and whisk until combined on medium-low heat. This should only take 1–2 minutes
6. Install a crisper plate in both drawers. Place half the meatloaf in the zone 1 drawer and half in zone 2's, then insert the drawers into the unit.
7. Select zone 1, select AIR FRY, set temperature to 390°F, and set time to 25 minutes. Select MATCH to match zone 2 settings to zone 1. Press the START/STOP button to begin cooking.
8. When the time reaches 20 minutes, press START/STOP to pause the unit. Remove the drawers and coat the meatloaf with the sauce using a brush. Re-insert the drawers into the unit and press START/STOP to resume cooking.
9. Carefully remove and serve.

Serving Suggestion: Serve with salad or fried quinoa.
Variation Tip: You can use ground pork instead.
Nutritional Information Per Serving:
Calories 727 | Fat 34g | Sodium 688mg | Carbs 57g | Fiber 3g | Sugar 34g | Protein 49g

Parmesan Pork Chops

Prep Time: 5 minutes
Cook Time: 20 minutes
Serves: 4
Ingredients:
• 4 boneless pork chops
• 2 tablespoons extra-virgin olive oil
• ½ cup freshly grated parmesan
• 1 teaspoon kosher salt
• 1 teaspoon paprika
• 1 teaspoon garlic powder
• 1 teaspoon onion powder
• ½ teaspoon freshly ground black pepper
Preparation:
1. Dry the pork chops with paper towels before brushing both sides with oil.
2. Combine the parmesan and spices in a medium mixing bowl. Coat the pork chops on both sides with the parmesan mixture.
3. Install a crisper plate in both drawers. Place half the pork chops in the zone 1 drawer and half in zone 2's, then insert the drawers into the unit.
1. Select zone 1, select AIR FRY, set temperature to 390°F, and set time to 20 minutes. Select MATCH to match zone 2 settings to zone 1. Press the START/STOP button to begin cooking.
2. When the time reaches 10 minutes, press START/STOP to pause the unit. Remove the drawers and flip the chicken. Re-insert the drawers into the unit and press START/STOP to resume cooking.
Serving Suggestion: Serve the pork chops with veggies.
Variation Tip: Use any kind of cheese you prefer.
Nutritional Information Per Serving:
Calories 199 | Fat 10.8g | Sodium 663mg | Carbs 1.6g | Fiber 0.4g | Sugar 0.4g | Protein 23.9g

Korean BBQ Beef

Prep Time: 15 minutes
Cook Time: 30 minutes
Serves: 6
Ingredients:
For the meat:
• 1 pound flank steak or thinly sliced steak
• ¼ cup corn starch
• Coconut oil spray
For the sauce:
• ½ cup soy sauce or gluten-free soy sauce
• ½ cup brown sugar
• 2 tablespoons white wine vinegar
• 1 clove garlic, crushed
• 1 tablespoon hot chili sauce
• 1 teaspoon ground ginger
• ½ teaspoon sesame seeds
• 1 tablespoon corn starch
• 1 tablespoon water
Preparation:
1. To begin, prepare the steak. Thinly slice it in that toss it in the corn starch to be coated thoroughly. Spray the tops with some coconut oil.
2. Spray the crisping plates and drawers with the coconut oil.
3. Place the crisping plates into the drawers. Place the steak strips into each drawer. Insert both drawers into the unit.
4. Select zone 1, Select AIR FRY, set the temperature to 375°F, and set time to 30 minutes. Select MATCH to match zone 2 settings with zone 1. Press the START/STOP button to begin cooking.
5. While the steak is cooking, add the sauce Ingredients: EXCEPT for the corn starch and water to a medium saucepan.
6. Warm it up to a low boil, then whisk in the corn starch and water.
7. Carefully remove the steak and pour the sauce over. Mix well.
Serving Suggestion: Serve with rice and steamed veggies.
Variation Tip: You can use potato starch instead of corn starch.
Nutritional Information Per Serving:
Calories 500 | Fat 19.8g | Sodium 680mg | Carbs 50.1g | Fiber 4.1g | Sugar 0g | Protein 27.9g

Tomahawk Steak

Prep Time: 20 minutes
Cook Time: 12 minutes
Serves: 4
Ingredients:
• 4 tablespoons butter, softened
• 2 cloves garlic, minced
• 2 teaspoons chopped fresh parsley
• 1 teaspoon chopped chives
• 1 teaspoon chopped fresh thyme
• 1 teaspoon chopped fresh rosemary
• 2 (2 pounds each) bone-in ribeye steaks
• Kosher salt, to taste
• Freshly ground black pepper, to taste
Preparation:
1. In a small bowl, combine the butter and herbs. Place the mixture in the center of a piece of plastic wrap and roll it into a log. Twist the ends together to keep it tight and refrigerate until hardened, about 20 minutes.
2. Season the steaks on both sides with salt and pepper.
3. Install a crisper plate in both drawers. Place one steak in the zone 1 drawer and one in zone 2's, then insert the drawers into the unit.
4. Select zone 1, select AIR FRY, set temperature to 390°F, and set time to 12 minutes. Select MATCH to match zone 2 settings to zone 1. Press the START/STOP button to begin cooking.
5. When the time reaches 10 minutes, press START/STOP to pause the unit. Remove the drawers and flip the steaks. Add the herb-butter to the tops of the steaks. Re-insert the drawers into the unit and press START/STOP to resume cooking.
6. Serve and enjoy!
Serving Suggestion: Serve with fries and a salad.
Variation Tip: You can add seasonings of your choice.
Nutritional Information Per Serving:
Calories 338 | Fat 21.2g | Sodium 1503mg | Carbs 5.1g | Fiber 0.3g | Sugar 4.6g | Protein 29.3g

Steak Fajitas With Onions and Peppers

Prep Time: 10 minutes
Cook Time: 15 minutes
Serves: 6

Ingredients:
• 1 pound steak
• 1 green bell pepper, sliced
• 1 yellow bell pepper, sliced
• 1 red bell pepper, sliced
• ½ cup sliced white onions
• 1 packet gluten-free fajita seasoning
• Olive oil spray

Preparation:
1. Thinly slice the steak against the grain. These should be about ¼-inch slices.
2. Mix the steak with the peppers and onions.
3. Evenly coat with the fajita seasoning.
4. Install a crisper plate in both drawers. Place half the steak mixture in the zone 1 drawer and half in zone 2's, then insert the drawers into the unit.
5. Select zone 1, select AIR FRY, set temperature to 390°F, and set time to 15 minutes. Select MATCH to match zone 2 settings to zone 1. Press the START/STOP button to begin cooking.
6. When the time reaches 10 minutes, press START/STOP to pause the unit. Remove the drawers and flip the steak strips. Re-insert the drawers into the unit and press START/STOP to resume cooking.
7. Serve in warm tortillas.

Serving Suggestion: Serve with guacamole and salsa.
Variation Tip: You can use pork strips instead.
Nutritional Information Per Serving:
Calories 305 | Fat 17g | Sodium 418mg | Carbs 15g | Fiber 2g | Sugar 4g | Protein 22g

Short Ribs & Root Vegetables

Prep Time: 15 Minutes
Cook Time: 45 Minutes
Serves: 2

Ingredients:
• 1 pound beef short ribs, bone-in and trimmed
• Salt and black pepper, to taste
• 2 tablespoons canola oil, divided
• ¼ cup red wine
• 3 tablespoons brown sugar
• 2 cloves garlic, peeled, minced
• 4 carrots, peeled, cut into 1-inch pieces
• 2 parsnips, peeled, cut into 1-inch pieces
• ½ cup pearl onions

Preparation:
1. Season the ribs with salt and black pepper and rub a small amount of canola oil on both sides.
2. Place the ribs in zone 1 basket of the air fryer.
3. Next, take a bowl and add the pearl onions, parsnips, carrots, garlic, brown sugar, red wine, salt, and black pepper.
4. Add the vegetable mixture to the zone 2 basket.
5. Press the Sync button.
6. Hit START/STOP button so the cooking cycle begins.
7. Once the cooking is complete, take out and serve.
8. Enjoy it hot.

Serving Suggestion: Serve it with mashed potatoes
Variation Tip: Use olive oil instead of canola oil
Nutritional Information Per Serving:
Calories 1262 | Fat 98.6g| Sodium 595mg | Carbs 57g | Fiber 10.1g| Sugar 28.2g | Protein 35.8g

Ham Burger Patties

Prep Time: 15 Minutes
Cook Time: 17 Minutes
Serves: 2

Ingredients:
• 1 pound ground beef
• Salt and pepper, to taste
• ½ teaspoon red chili powder
• ¼ teaspoon coriander powder
• 2 tablespoons chopped onion
• 1 green chili, chopped
• Oil spray for greasing
• 2 large potato wedges

Preparation:
1. Grease the air fryer baskets with oil.
2. Place the potato wedges into the zone 1 basket.
3. Add the minced beef, salt, pepper, chili powder, coriander powder, green chili, and chopped onion to a bowl and mix well.
4. With wet hands, make two burger patties out of the mixture and place in zone 2 of the air fryer.
5. Set the time for zone 1 to 12 minutes on AIR FRY mode at 400 degrees F.
6. Select the MATCH button for zone 2.
7. Once the time is up, take the baskets out and flip the patties and shake the potato wedges.
8. Set zone 1 for 4 minutes at 400 degrees F on AIR FRY.
9. Select the MATCH button for the second basket.
10. Once it's done, serve and enjoy.

Serving Suggestion: Serve with bread slices, cheese, pickles, lettuce, and onions
Variation Tip: None
Nutritional Information Per Serving:
Calories 875 | Fat 21.5g | Sodium 622mg | Carbs 88g | Fiber 10.9 g| Sugar 3.4g | Protein 78.8g

Chinese BBQ Pork

Prep Time: 15 Minutes
Cook Time: 25-35 Minutes
Serves: 2

Ingredients:
• 4 tablespoons soy sauce
• ¼ cup red wine
• 2 tablespoons oyster sauce
• ¼ tablespoon hoisin sauce
• ¼ cup honey
• ¼ cup brown sugar
• Pinch of salt
• Pinch of black pepper
• 1 teaspoon ginger garlic, paste
• 1 teaspoon five-spice powder

Other Ingredients:
• 1.5 pounds pork shoulder, sliced

Preparation:
1. Take a bowl and mix all the sauce Ingredients: well.
2. Transfer half of it to a sauce pan and cook for 10 minutes, and then set it aside.
3. Let the pork marinate in the remaining sauce for 2 hours.
4. Place the pork slices in the air fryer basket in zone 1 and set it to AIR FRY mode at 450 degrees F for 25 minutes.
5. Make sure the internal temperature is above 160 degrees F once cooked.
6. If not, add a few more minutes to the overall cooking time.
7. Once done, take it out and baste it with the cooked sauce.
8. Serve and Enjoy.

Serving Suggestion: Serve it with rice
Variation Tip: Skip the wine and add vinegar
Nutritional Information Per Serving:
Calories 1239| Fat 73 g| Sodium 2185 mg | Carbs 57.3 g | Fiber 0.4g| Sugar 53.7 g | Protein 81.5 g

Yogurt Lamb Chops

Prep Time: 10 Minutes
Cook Time: 20 Minutes
Serves: 2
Ingredients:
• 1½ cups plain Greek yogurt
• 1 lemon, juice only
• 1 teaspoon ground cumin
• 1 teaspoon ground coriander
• ¾ teaspoon ground turmeric
• ¼ teaspoon ground allspice
• 10 rib lamb chops (1–1¼ inches thick cut)
• 2 tablespoons olive oil, divided
Preparation:
1. In a bowl, add all the Ingredients: and rub the chops well. Let it marinate for an hour in the refrigerator.
2. After an hour take out the chops and layer the air fryer baskets with parchment paper.
3. Divide the chops between both the baskets.
4. Set the time for zone 1 to 20 minutes at 400 degrees F on AIR FRY.
5. Select the MATCH button for the zone 2 basket.
6. Hit START/STOP button and then wait for the chops to cook.
7. Once done, serve and enjoy.
Serving Suggestion: Serve over rice
Variation Tip: Use canola oil instead of olive oil
Nutritional Information Per Serving:
Calories 1206 | Fat 66.7 g| Sodium 478mg | Carbs 10.6g | Fiber 1.2g | Sugar 6g | Protein 132.8g

Garlic Butter Steaks

Prep Time: 120 minutes
Cook Time: 25 minutes
Serves: 2
Ingredients:
• 2 (6 ounces each) sirloin steaks or ribeyes
• 2 tablespoons unsalted butter
• 1 clove garlic, crushed
• ½ teaspoon dried parsley
• ½ teaspoon dried rosemary
• Salt and pepper, to taste
Preparation:
1. Season the steaks with salt and pepper and set them to rest for about 2 hours before cooking.
2. Put the butter in a bowl. Add the garlic, parsley, and rosemary. Allow the butter to soften.
3. Whip together with a fork or spoon once the butter has softened.
4. When you're ready to cook, install a crisper plate in both drawers. Place the sirloin steaks in a single layer in each drawer. Insert the drawers into the unit.
5. Select zone 1, select AIR FRY, set temperature to 360°F, and set time to 10 minutes. Select MATCH to match zone 2 settings to zone 1. Select START/STOP to begin.
6. Once done, serve with the garlic butter.
Serving Suggestion: Serve with a side salad.
Variation Tip: You can use garlic powder instead of fresh.
Nutritional Information Per Serving:
Calories 519 | Fat 36g | Sodium 245mg | Carbs 1g | Fiber 0g | Sugar 0g | Protein 46g

Rosemary and Garlic Lamb Chops

Prep Time: 10 minutes (plus 1 hour for marinating)
Cook Time: 15 minutes
Serves: 4

Ingredients:
• 8 lamb chops
• 3 tablespoons olive oil
• 2 tablespoons chopped fresh rosemary
• 1 teaspoon garlic powder or 3 cloves garlic, minced
• 1 teaspoon salt, or to taste
• ½ teaspoon black pepper, or to taste

Preparation:
1. Dry the lamb chops with a paper towel.
2. Combine the olive oil, rosemary, garlic, salt, and pepper in a large mixing bowl. Toss the lamb in the marinade gently to coat it. Cover and set aside to marinate for 1 hour or up to overnight.
3. Install a crisper plate in both drawers. Place half the lamb chops in the zone 1 drawer and half in zone 2's, then insert the drawers into the unit.
4. Select zone 1, select AIR FRY, set temperature to 390°F, and set time to 15 minutes. Select MATCH to match zone 2 settings to zone 1. Press the START/STOP button to begin cooking.
5. When the time reaches 10 minutes, press START/STOP to pause the unit. Remove the drawers and flip the chops. Re-insert the drawers into the unit and press START/STOP to resume cooking.
6. Serve and enjoy!

Serving Suggestion: Serve with mashed potatoes.
Variation Tip: You can use other seasonings of your choice.
Nutritional Information Per Serving:
Calories 427 | Fat 34g | Sodium 668mg | Carbs 1g | Fiber 1g | Sugar 1g | Protein 31g

Roast Beef

Prep Time: 5 minutes
Cook Time: 35 minutes
Serves: 4

Ingredients:
• 2 pounds beef roast
• 1 tablespoon olive oil
• 1 medium onion (optional)
• 1 teaspoon salt
• 2 teaspoons rosemary and thyme, chopped (fresh or dried)

Preparation:
1. Combine the sea salt, rosemary, and oil in a large, shallow dish.
2. Using paper towels, pat the meat dry. Place it on a dish and turn it to coat the outside with the oil-herb mixture.
3. Peel the onion and split it in half (if using).
4. Install a crisper plate in both drawers. Place half the beef roast and half an onion in the zone 1 drawer and half the beef and half the onion in zone 2's, then insert the drawers into the unit.
5. Select zone 1, select AIR FRY, set temperature to 360°F, and set time to 22 minutes. Select MATCH to match zone 2 settings to zone 1. Press the START/STOP button to begin cooking.
6. When the time reaches 11 minutes, press START/STOP to pause the unit. Remove the drawers and flip the roast. Re-insert the drawers into the unit and press START/STOP to resume cooking.

Serving Suggestion: Serve with roasted veggies.
Variation Tip: You can use pork instead.
Nutritional Information Per Serving:
Calories 463 | Fat 17.8g | Sodium 732mg | Carbs 2.8g | Fiber 0.7g | Sugar 1.2g | Protein 69g

Bell Peppers with Sausages

Prep Time: 15 Minutes
Cook Time: 20 Minutes
Serves: 4

Ingredients:
- 6 beef or pork Italian sausages
- 4 bell peppers, whole
- Oil spray, for greasing
- 2 cups cooked rice
- 1 cup sour cream

Preparation:
1. Put the bell peppers in the zone 1 basket and sausages in the zone 2 basket of the air fryer.
2. Set zone 1 to AIR FRY mode for 10 minutes at 400 degrees F.
3. For zone 2 set it to 20 minutes at 375 degrees F.
4. Hit the Sync button, so both finish at the same time.
5. After 5 minutes, take out the sausage basket and break or mince it with a plastic spatula and then place it back in.
6. Once done, serve the minced meat with bell peppers and serve over cooked rice with a dollop of sour cream.

Serving Suggestion: Serve it with salad
Variation Tip: Use olive oil instead of oil spray
Nutritional Information Per Serving:
Calories 737 | Fat 21.1g| Sodium 124mg | Carbs 85.4g | Fiber 2.8g | Sugar 6.2g | Protein 48.2g

Chapter 7 Dessert Recipes

Fudge Brownies

Prep Time: 20 Minutes
Cook Time: 16 Minutes
Serves: 4
Ingredients:
• ½ cup all-purpose flour
• ¼ cup unsweetened cocoa powder
• ¾ teaspoon kosher salt
• 2 large eggs, whisked
• 1 tablespoon almond milk
• ½ cup brown sugar
• ½ cup packed white sugar
• ½ tablespoon vanilla extract
• 8 ounces semisweet chocolate chips, melted
• ½ cup unsalted butter, melted
Preparation:
1. Take a medium bowl, and use a hand beater to whisk together eggs, milk, both the sugars and vanilla.
2. In a separate microwave-safe bowl, mix the melted butter and chocolate and microwave it for 30 seconds to melt the chocolate.
3. Add all the dry Ingredients: to the chocolate mixture.
4. Slowly add the egg mixture to the bowl.
Spray a reasonable round baking pan and pour the batter into the pan.
5. Select the AIR FRY mode and adjust the setting the temperature to 300 degrees F, for 30 minutes.
6. Check it after 30 minutes and if not done, cook for 10 more minutes.
7. Once it's done, take it out and let it cool before serving.
8. Enjoy.
Serving Suggestion: Serve it with a dollop of the vanilla ice cream
Variation Tip: Use dairy milk instead of almond milk
Nutritional Information Per Serving:
Calories 760| Fat 43.3 g| Sodium 644mg | Carbs 93.2g | Fiber 5.3g | Sugar 70.2g | Protein 6.2g

Chocolate Chip Cake

Prep Time: 12 Minutes
Cook Time: 15 Minutes
Serves: 4
Ingredients:
• Salt, pinch
• 2 eggs, whisked
• ½ cup brown sugar
• ½ cup butter, melted
• 10 tablespoons almond milk
• ¼ teaspoon vanilla extract
• ½ teaspoon baking powder
• 1 cup all-purpose flour
• 1 cup chocolate chips
• ½ cup cocoa powder
Preparation:
1. Take 2 round baking pans that fit inside the baskets of the air fryer and line them with baking paper.
2. In a bowl with an electric beater, mix the eggs, brown sugar, butter, almond milk, and vanilla extract.
3. In a second bowl, mix the flour, cocoa powder, baking powder, and salt.
4. Slowly add the dry Ingredients: to the wet Ingredients:.
5. Fold in the chocolate chips and mix well with a spoon or spatula.
6. Divide this batter into the round baking pans.
7. Set the time for zone 1 to 16 minutes at 350 degrees F on AIR FRY mode.
8. Select the MATCH button for the zone 2 basket.
9. After the time is up, check.   If they're not done, let them AIR FRY for one more minute.
10. Once it is done, serve.
Serving Suggestion: Serve it with chocolate syrup drizzle
Variation Tip: Use baking soda instead of baking powder
Nutritional Information Per Serving:
Calories 736| Fat 45.5g| Sodium 356mg | Carbs 78.2g | Fiber 6.1g | Sugar 32.7g | Protein 11.5 g

Mini Strawberry and Cream Pies

Prep Time: 12 Minutes
Cook Time: 10 Minutes
Serves: 2
Ingredients:
• 1 box store-bought pie dough, Trader Joe's
• 1 cup strawberries, cubed
• 3 tablespoons cream, heavy
• 2 tablespoons almonds
• 1 egg white, for brushing
Preparation:
1. Take the store-bought pie dough and flatten it on a surface.
2. Use a round cutter to cut it into 3-inch circles.
3. Brush the dough with egg white all around the edges.
4. Now add almonds, strawberries, and cream in a tiny amount in the center of the dough, and top it with another dough circle.
5. Press the edges with a fork to seal it.
6. Make a slit in the middle of the pie and divide them into the baskets.
7. Set zone 1 to AIR FRY mode 360 degrees F for 10 minutes.
8. Select MATCH for zone 2 basket.
9. Once done, serve.
Serving Suggestion: Serve it with vanilla ice-cream
Variation Tip: Use orange zest instead of lemon zest
Nutritional Information Per Serving:
Calories 203| Fat 12.7g| Sodium 193mg | Carbs 20g | Fiber 2.2g | Sugar 5.8g | Protein 3.7g

Mini Blueberry Pies

Prep Time: 12 Minutes
Cook Time: 10 Minutes
Serves: 2
Ingredients:
• 1 box store-bought pie dough, Trader Joe's
• ¼ cup blueberry jam
• 1 teaspoon lemon zest
• 1 egg white, for brushing
Preparation:
1. Take the store-bought pie dough and cut it into 3-inch circles.
2. Brush the dough with egg white all around the edges.
3. Now add blueberry jam and zest in the middle and top it with another circle.
4. Press the edges with a fork to seal it.
5. Make a slit in the middle of each pie and divide them between the baskets.
6. Set zone 1 to AIR FRY mode 360 degrees for 10 minutes.
7. Select the MATCH button for zone 2.
8. Once cooked, serve.
Serving Suggestion: Serve it with vanilla ice-cream
Variation Tip: Use orange zest instead of lemon zest
Nutritional Information Per Serving:
Calories 234| Fa t8.6g| Sodium 187 mg | Carbs 38.2 g | Fiber 0.1g | Sugar 13.7g | Protein 2g

Air Fried Bananas

Prep Time: 10 minutes.
Cook Time: 13 minutes.
Serves: 4
Ingredients:
• 4 bananas, sliced
• 1 avocado oil cooking spray
Preparation:
1. Spread the banana slices in the two crisper plates in a single layer.
2. Drizzle avocado oil over the banana slices.
3. Return the crisper plate to the Ninja Foodi Dual Zone Air Fryer.
4. Choose the Air Fry mode for Zone 1 and set the temperature to 350 degrees F and the time to 13 minutes.
5. Select the "MATCH" button to copy the settings for Zone 2.
6. Initiate cooking by pressing the START/STOP button.
7. Serve.
Serving Suggestion: Serve with a dollop of vanilla ice-cream.
Variation Tip: Drizzle chopped nuts on top of the bananas.
Nutritional Information Per Serving:
Calories 149 | Fat 1.2g |Sodium 3mg | Carbs 37.6g | Fiber 5.8g | Sugar 29g | Protein 1.1g

Grilled Peaches

Prep Time: 5minutes
Cook Time: 10 minutes
Serves: 4

Ingredients:
- 2 yellow peaches
- ¼ cup graham cracker crumbs
- ¼ cup brown sugar
- ¼ cup butter, diced into tiny cubes
- Whipped cream or ice cream, for serving.

Preparation:
1. Cut the peaches into wedges and pull out their pits.
2. Install a crisper plate in both drawers. Put half of the peach wedges into the drawer in zone 1 and half in zone 2's. Sprinkle the tops of the wedges with the crumbs, sugar, and butter. Insert the drawers into the unit.
3. Select zone 1, select AIR FRY, set the temperature to 390°F, and set the time to 10 minutes. Select MATCH to match zone 2 settings to zone 1. Press the START/STOP button to begin cooking.

Serving Suggestion: Serve the peaches with whipped cream or ice cream.

Variation Tip: You can use apples if you prefer.

Nutritional Information Per Serving:
Calories 200 | Fat 13.2g | Sodium 132mg | Carbs 20.1g | Fiber 1.3g | Sugar 16.8g | Protein 1.3g

Bread Pudding

Prep Time: 12 Minutes
Cook Time: 8-12 Minutes
Serves: 2

Ingredients:
- Nonstick spray, for greasing ramekins
- 2 slices of white bread, crumbled
- 4 tablespoons white sugar
- 5 large eggs
- ½ cup cream
- Salt, pinch
- ⅓ teaspoon cinnamon powder

Preparation:
1. Take a bowl and whisk eggs in it.
2. Add sugar and salt to the eggs and whisk it all well.
3. Then add cream and use a hand beater to incorporate the Ingredients:.

4. Next add cinnamon, and the crumbled white bread.
5. Mix it well and add into two round shaped baking pans.
6. Place each baking pan in the air fryer basket.
7. Set zone 1 to AIR FRY mode at 350 degrees F for 8-12 minutes.
8. Press MATCH button for zone 2.
9. Once it's cooked, serve.

Serving Suggestion: Serve it with coffee
Variation Tip: Use brown sugar instead of white sugar
Nutritional Information Per Serving:
Calories 331| Fat 16.1g| Sodium 331mg | Carbs 31g | Fiber 0.2g | Sugar 26.2g | Protein 16.2g

Lemony Sweet Twists

Prep Time: 15 Minutes
Cook Time: 9 Minutes
Serves: 2

Ingredients:
- 1 box store-bought puff pastry
- ½ teaspoon lemon zest
- 1 tablespoon lemon juice
- 2 teaspoons brown sugar
- Salt, pinch
- 2 tablespoons Parmesan cheese, freshly grated

Preparation:
1. Put the puff pastry dough on a clean work surface.
2. In a bowl, combine Parmesan cheese, brown sugar, salt, lemon zest, and lemon juice.
3. Press this mixture into both sides of the dough.
4. Now, cut the pastry into 1" x 4" strips.
5. Twist 2 times from each end.
6. Place the strips into the air fryer baskets.
7. Select zone 1 to AIR FRY mode at 400 degrees F for 9-10 minutes.
8. Select MATCH for zone 2 basket.
9. Once cooked, serve and enjoy.

Serving Suggestion: Serve them with champagne
Variation Tip: None
Nutritional Information Per Serving:
Calories 156| Fat 10g| Sodium 215mg | Carbs 14g | Fiber 0.4g | Sugar 3.3g | Protein 2.8g

Lava Cake

Prep Time: 10 minutes
Cook Time: 10 minutes
Serves: 4
Ingredients:
• 1 cup semi-sweet chocolate chips
• 8 tablespoons butter
• 4 eggs
• 2 teaspoons vanilla extract
• ½ teaspoon salt
• 6 tablespoons all-purpose flour
• 1 cup powdered sugar
For the chocolate filling:
• 2 tablespoons Nutella
• 1 tablespoon butter, softened
• 1 tablespoon powdered sugar
Preparation:
1. Heat the chocolate chips and butter in a medium-sized microwave-safe bowl in 30-second intervals until thoroughly melted and smooth, stirring after each interval.
2. Whisk together the eggs, vanilla, salt, flour, and powdered sugar in a mixing bowl.
3. Combine the Nutella, softened butter, and powdered sugar in a separate bowl.
4. Spray 4 ramekins with oil and fill them halfway with the chocolate chip mixture. Fill each ramekin halfway with Nutella, then top with the remaining chocolate chip mixture, making sure the Nutella is well covered.
5. Install a crisper plate in both drawers. Place 2 ramekins in each drawer and insert the drawers into the unit.
6. Select zone 1, select AIR FRY, set temperature to 390°F, and set time to 22 minutes. Select MATCH to match zone 2 settings to zone 1. Press the START/STOP button to begin cooking.
7. Serve hot.
Serving Suggestion: Serve with a sprinkling of powdered sugar and a scoop of vanilla ice cream.
Variation Tip: You can use a mixture of semi-sweet and dark chocolate.
Nutritional Information Per Serving:
Calories 338 | Fat 21.2g | Sodium 1503mg | Carbs 5.1g | Fiber 0.3g | Sugar 4.6g | Protein 29.3g

Strawberry Nutella Hand Pies

Prep Time: 20 minutes
Cook Time: 10 minutes
Serves: 8
Ingredients:
• 1 tube pie crust dough
• 3–4 strawberries, finely chopped
• Nutella
• Sugar
• Coconut oil cooking spray
Preparation:
1. Roll out the pie dough and place it on a baking sheet. Cut out hearts using a 3-inch heart-shaped cookie cutter as precisely as possible.
2. Gather the leftover dough into a ball and roll it out thinly to make a few more heart shapes. For 8 hand pies, I was able to get 16 hearts from one tube of pie crust.
3. Set aside a baking tray lined with parchment paper.
4. Spread a dollop of Nutella (approximately 1 teaspoon) on one of the hearts. Add a few strawberry pieces to the mix. Add a pinch of sugar to the top.
5. Place another heart on top and use a fork to tightly crimp the edges. Gently poke holes in the top of the pie with a fork. Place on a baking sheet. Repeat for all the pies.
6. All of the pies on the tray should be sprayed with coconut oil.
7. Install a crisper plate in both drawers. Place half the pies in the zone 1 drawer and half in zone 2's, then insert the drawers into the unit.
8. Select zone 1, select BAKE, set temperature to 390°F, and set time to 10 minutes. Select MATCH to match zone 2 settings to zone 1. Press the START/STOP button to begin cooking.
Serving Suggestion: Serve with ice cream.
Variation Tip: You can use your choice of berries.
Nutritional Information Per Serving:
Calories 41 | Fat 2.1g | Sodium 18mg | Carbs 5.5g | Fiber 0.4g | Sugar 4.1g | Protein 0.4g

Churros

Prep Time: 10 minutes
Cook Time: 10 minutes
Serves: 8

Ingredients:
- 1 cup water
- $1/3$ cup unsalted butter, cut into cubes
- 2 tablespoons granulated sugar
- ¼ teaspoon salt
- 1 cup all-purpose flour
- 2 large eggs
- 1 teaspoon vanilla extract
- Cooking oil spray

For the cinnamon-sugar coating:
- ½ cup granulated sugar
- ¾ teaspoon ground cinnamon

Preparation:
1. Add the water, butter, sugar, and salt to a medium pot. Bring to a boil over medium-high heat.
2. Reduce the heat to medium-low and stir in the flour. Cook, stirring constantly with a rubber spatula until the dough is smooth and comes together.
3. Remove the dough from the heat and place it in a mixing bowl. Allow 4 minutes for cooling.
4. In a mixing bowl, beat the eggs and vanilla extract with an electric hand mixer or stand mixer until the dough comes together. The finished product will resemble gluey mashed potatoes. Press the lumps together into a ball with your hands, then transfer to a large piping bag with a large star-shaped tip. Pipe out the churros.
5. Install a crisper plate in both drawers. Place half the churros in the zone 1 drawer and half in zone 2's, then insert the drawers into the unit.
6. Select zone 1, select AIR FRY, set temperature to 390°F, and set time to 12 minutes. Select MATCH to match zone 2 settings to zone 1. Press the START/STOP button to begin cooking.
7. In a shallow bowl, combine the granulated sugar and cinnamon.
8. Immediately transfer the baked churros to the bowl with the sugar mixture and toss to coat.

Serving Suggestion: Serve warm with Nutella or chocolate dipping sauce.

Variation Tip: You can use coconut flour instead.
Nutritional Information Per Serving:
Calories 204 | Fat 9g | Sodium 91mg | Carbs 27g | Fiber 0.3g | Sugar 15g | Protein 3g

Cinnamon Sugar Dessert Fries

Prep Time: 5 minutes
Cook Time: 15 minutes
Serves: 4

Ingredients:
- 2 sweet potatoes
- 1 tablespoon butter, melted
- 1 teaspoon butter, melted
- 2 tablespoons sugar
- ½ teaspoon ground cinnamon

Preparation:
1. Peel and cut the sweet potatoes into skinny fries.
2. Coat the fries with 1 tablespoon of butter.
3. Install a crisper plate into each drawer. Place half the sweet potatoes in the zone 1 drawer and half in zone 2's, then insert the drawers into the unit.
4. Select zone 1, select AIR FRY, set temperature to 390°F, and set time to 15 minutes. Select MATCH to match zone 2 settings to zone 1. Press the START/STOP button to begin cooking.
5. When the time reaches 11 minutes, press START/STOP to pause the unit. Remove the drawers and flip the fries. Re-insert the drawers into the unit and press START/STOP to resume cooking.
6. Meanwhile, mix the 1 teaspoon of butter, the sugar, and the cinnamon in a large bowl.
7. When the fries are done, add them to the bowl, and toss them to coat.
8. Serve and enjoy!

Serving Suggestion: Serve with chocolate dipping sauce.
Variation Tip: You can add a pinch of ground nutmeg.
Nutritional Information Per Serving:
Calories 110 | Fat 4g | Sodium 51mg | Carbs 18g | Fiber 2g | Sugar 10g | Protein 1g

Apple Fritters

Prep Time: 10 minutes
Cook Time: 10 minutes
Serves: 14
Ingredients:
• 2 large apples
• 2 cups all-purpose flour
• ½ cup granulated sugar
• 1 tablespoon baking powder
• 1 teaspoon salt
• 1 teaspoon ground cinnamon
• ½ teaspoon ground nutmeg
• ¼ teaspoon ground cloves
• ¾ cup apple cider or apple juice
• 2 eggs
• 3 tablespoons butter, melted
• 1 teaspoon vanilla extract
For the apple cider glaze:
• 2 cups powdered sugar
• ¼ cup apple cider or apple juice
• ½ teaspoon ground cinnamon
• ¼ teaspoon ground nutmeg
Preparation:
1. Peel and core the apples, then cut them into ¼-inch cubes. Spread the apple chunks out on a kitchen towel to absorb any excess moisture.
2. In a mixing bowl, combine the flour, sugar, baking powder, salt, and spices.
3. Add the apple chunks and combine well.
4. Whisk together the apple cider, eggs, melted butter, and vanilla in a small bowl.
5. Combine the wet and dry Ingredients: in a large mixing bowl.
6. Install a crisper plate in both drawers. Use an ice cream scoop to scoop 3 to 4 dollops of fritter dough into the zone 1 drawer and 3 to 4 dollops into the zone 2 drawer. Insert the drawers into the unit. You may need to cook in batches.
7. Select zone 1, select BAKE, set temperature to 390°F, and set time to 10 minutes. Select MATCH to match zone 2 settings to zone 1. Press the START/STOP button to begin cooking.
8. Meanwhile, make the glaze: Whisk the powdered sugar, apple cider, and spices together until smooth.
9. When the fritters are cooked, drizzle the glaze over them. Let sit for 10 minutes until the glaze sets.
Serving Suggestion: Serve with your favorite hot beverage.
Variation Tip: You can use pears instead.
Nutritional Information Per Serving:
Calories 221 | Fat 3g | Sodium 288mg | Carbs 46g | Fiber 2g | Sugar 29g | Protein 3g

Fried Oreos

Prep Time: 2 minutes
Cook Time: 8 minutes
Serves: 8
Ingredients:
• 1 can Pillsbury Crescent Dough (or equivalent)
• 8 Oreo cookies
• 1–2 tablespoons powdered sugar
Preparation:
1. Open the crescent dough up and cut it into the right-size pieces to completely wrap each cookie.
2. Wrap each Oreo in dough. Make sure that there are no air bubbles and that the cookies are completely covered.
3. Install a crisper plate in both drawers. Place half the Oreo cookies in the zone 1 drawer and half in zone 2's. Sprinkle the tops with the powdered sugar, then insert the drawers into the unit.
4. Select zone 1, select AIR FRY, set temperature to 390°F, and set time to 8 minutes. Select MATCH to match zone 2 settings to zone 1. Press the START/STOP button to begin cooking.
5. Serve warm and enjoy!
Serving Suggestion: Serve warm with vanilla ice cream and a dusting of powdered sugar.
Variation Tip: You can use brown sugar.
Nutritional Information Per Serving:
Calories 338 | Fat 21.2g | Sodium 1503mg | Carbs 5.1g | Fiber 0.3g | Sugar 4.6g | Protein 29.3g

Biscuit Doughnuts

Prep Time: 15 minutes.
Cook Time: 15 minutes.
Serves: 8

Ingredients:
- ½ cup white sugar
- 1 teaspoon cinnamon
- ½ cup powdered sugar
- 1 can pre-made biscuit dough
- Coconut oil
- Melted butter to brush biscuits

Preparation:
1. Place all the biscuits on a cutting board and cut holes in the center of each biscuit using a cookie cutter.
2. Grease the crisper plate with coconut oil.
3. Place the biscuits in the two crisper plates while keeping them 1 inch apart.
4. Return the crisper plates to the Ninja Foodi Dual Zone Air Fryer.
5. Choose the Air Fry mode for Zone 1 and set the temperature to 375 degrees F and the time to 15 minutes.
6. Select the "MATCH" button to copy the settings for Zone 2.
7. Initiate cooking by pressing the START/STOP button.
8. Brush all the donuts with melted butter and sprinkle cinnamon and sugar on top.
9. Air fry these donuts for one minute more.
10. Enjoy!

Serving Suggestion: Serve the doughnuts with chocolate syrup on top.
Variation Tip: Inject strawberry jam into each doughnut.
Nutritional Information Per Serving:
Calories 192 | Fat 9.3g |Sodium 133mg | Carbs 27.1g | Fiber 1.4g | Sugar 19g | Protein 3.2g

Oreo Rolls

Prep Time: 10 minutes.
Cook Time: 8 minutes.
Serves: 9

Ingredients:
- 1 crescent sheet roll
- 9 Oreo cookies
- Cinnamon powder, to serve
- Powdered sugar, to serve

Preparation:
1. Spread the crescent sheet roll and cut it into 9 equal squares.
2. Place one cookie at the center of each square.
3. Wrap each square around the cookies and press the ends to seal.
4. Place half of the wrapped cookies in each crisper plate.
5. Return the crisper plates to the Ninja Foodi Dual Zone Air Fryer.
6. Select the Bake mode for Zone 1 and set the temperature to 360 degrees F and the time to 4-6 minutes.
7. Select the "MATCH" button to copy the settings for Zone 2.
8. Initiate cooking by pressing the START/STOP button.
9. Check for the doneness of the cookie rolls if they are golden brown, else cook 1-2 minutes more.
10. Garnish the rolls with sugar and cinnamon.
11. Serve.

Serving Suggestion: Serve a cup of spice latte or hot chocolate.
Variation Tip: Dip the rolls in melted chocolate for a change of taste.
Nutritional Information Per Serving:
Calories 175 | Fat 13.1g |Sodium 154mg | Carbs 14g | Fiber 0.8g | Sugar 8.9g | Protein 0.7g

Apple Crisp

Prep Time: 15 minutes.
Cook Time: 14 minutes.
Serves: 8

Ingredients:
- 3 cups apples, chopped
- 1 tablespoon pure maple syrup
- 2 teaspoons lemon juice
- 3 tablespoons all-purpose flour
- ⅓ cup quick oats
- ¼ cup brown sugar
- 2 tablespoons light butter, melted
- ½ teaspoon cinnamon

Preparation:
1. Toss the chopped apples with 1 tablespoon of all-purpose flour, cinnamon, maple syrup, and lemon juice in a suitable bowl.
2. Divide the apples in the two air fryer baskets with their crisper plates.
3. Whisk oats, brown sugar, and remaining all-purpose flour in a small bowl.
4. Stir in melted butter, then divide this mixture over the apples.
5. Return the crisper plate to the Ninja Foodi Dual Zone Air Fryer.
6. Select the Bake mode for Zone 1 and set the temperature to 375 degrees F and the time to 14 minutes.
7. Select the "MATCH" button to copy the settings for Zone 2.
8. Initiate cooking by pressing the START/STOP button.
9. Enjoy fresh.

Serving Suggestion: Serve with a warming cup of hot chocolate.

Variation Tip: Use crushed cookies or graham crackers instead of oats.

Nutritional Information Per Serving:
Calories 258 | Fat 12.4g |Sodium 79mg | Carbs 34.3g | Fiber 1g | Sugar 17g | Protein 3.2g

Chocolate Chip Muffins

Prep Time: 12 Minutes
Cook Time: 15 Minutes
Serves: 2

Ingredients:
- Salt, pinch
- 2 eggs
- ⅓ cup brown sugar
- ⅓ cup butter
- 4 tablespoons milk
- ¼ teaspoon vanilla extract
- ½ teaspoon baking powder
- 1 cup all-purpose flour
- 1 pouch chocolate chips, 35 grams

Preparation:
1. Take 4 oven-safe ramekins that are the size of a cup and layer them with muffin papers.
2. In a bowl, with an electric beater mix the eggs, brown sugar, butter, milk, and vanilla extract.
3. In another bowl, mix the flour, baking powder, and salt.
4. Mix the dry Ingredients: into the wet Ingredients: slowly.
5. Fold in the chocolate chips and mix them in well.
6. Divide this batter into 4 ramekins and place them into both the baskets.
7. Set the time for zone 1 to 15 minutes at 350 degrees F on AIR FRY mode.
8. Select the MATCH button for the zone 2 basket.
9. If they are not completely done after 15 minutes, AIR FRY for another minute.
10. Once it is done, serve.

Serving Suggestion: Serve it with chocolate syrup drizzle

Variation Tip: None

Nutritional Information Per Serving:
Calories 757| Fat 40.3g| Sodium 426mg | Carbs 85.4g | Fiber 2.2g | Sugar 30.4g | Protein 14.4g

Pumpkin Muffins with Cinnamon

Prep Time: 20 Minutes
Cook Time: 20 Minutes
Serves: 4
Ingredients:
• 1 and ½ cups all-purpose flour
• ½ teaspoon baking soda
• ½ teaspoon baking powder
• 1 and ¼ teaspoons cinnamon, groaned
• ¼ teaspoon ground nutmeg, grated
• 2 large eggs
• Salt, pinch
• ¾ cup granulated sugar
• ½ cup dark brown sugar
• 1 and ½ cups pumpkin puree
• ¼ cup coconut milk
Preparation:
1. Take 4 ramekins and layer them with muffin paper.
2. In a bowl, add the eggs, brown sugar, baking soda, baking powder, cinnamon, nutmeg, and sugar and whisk well with an electric mixer.
3. In a second bowl, mix the flour, and salt.
4. Slowly add the dry Ingredients: to the wet Ingredients:.
5. Fold in the pumpkin puree and milk and mix it in well.
6. Divide this batter into 4 ramekins.
7. Place two ramekins in each air fryer basket.
8. Set the time for zone 1 to 18 minutes at 360 degrees on AIR FRY mode.
9. Select the MATCH button for the zone 2 basket.
10. Check after the time is up and if not done, and let it AIR FRY for one more minute.
11. Once it is done, serve.
Serving Suggestion: Serve it with a glass of milk
Variation Tip: Use almond milk instead of coconut milk
Nutritional Information Per Serving:
Calories 291| Fat 6.4g| Sodium 241mg | Carbs 57.1g | Fiber 4.4g | Sugar 42g | Protein 5.9g

Baked Apples

Prep Time: 5 minutes
Cook Time: 20 minutes
Serves: 4
Ingredients:
• 4 granny smith apples, halved and cored
• ¼ cup old-fashioned oats (not the instant kind)
• 1 tablespoon butter, melted
• 2 tablespoon brown sugar
• ½ teaspoon ground cinnamon
• Whipped cream, for topping (optional)
Preparation:
1. Insert the crisper plates into the drawers. Lay the cored apple halves in a single layer into each of the drawers (the apple's flesh should be pointing up). Insert the drawers into the unit.
2. Select zone 1, select AIR FRY, set temperature to 350°F, and set time to 10 minutes. Select MATCH to match zone 2 settings to zone 1. Press the START/STOP button to begin cooking.
3. Meanwhile, mix the oats, melted butter, brown sugar, and cinnamon to form the topping.
4. Add the topping to the apple halves when they've cooked for 10 minutes.
5. Select zone 1, select BAKE, set temperature to 390°F, and set time to 22 minutes. Select MATCH to match zone 2 settings to zone 1. Press the START/STOP button to begin cooking.
6. Serve warm and enjoy!
Serving Suggestion: Serve with whipped cream or vanilla ice cream.
Variation Tip: You can use pears instead.
Nutritional Information Per Serving:
Calories 98 | Fat 3g | Sodium 25mg | Carbs 17g | Fiber 2g | Sugar 11g | Protein 1g

Air Fryer Sweet Twists

Prep Time: 15 Minutes
Cook Time: 9 Minutes
Serves: 2
Ingredients:
• 1 box store-bought puff pastry
• ½ teaspoon cinnamon
• ½ teaspoon sugar
• ½ teaspoon black sesame seeds
• Salt, pinch
• 2 tablespoons Parmesan cheese, freshly grated
Preparation:
1. Place the dough on a work surface.
2. Take a small bowl and mix in cheese, sugar, salt, sesame seeds, and cinnamon.
3. Press this mixture on both sides of the dough.
4. Now, cut the pastry into 1" x 3" strips.
5. Twist each of the strips twice from each end.
6. Transfer them to both the air fryer baskets.
7. Select zone 1 to AIR FRY mode at 400 degrees F for 9-10 minutes.
8. Select the MATCH button for the zone 2 basket.
9. Once cooked, serve.
Serving Suggestion: Serve it with champagne
Variation Tip: None
Nutritional Information Per Serving:
Calories 140| Fat9.4g| Sodium 142mg | Carbs 12.3g | Fiber 0.8 g | Sugar 1.2g | Protein 2g

Jelly Donuts

Prep Time: 5 minutes
Cook Time: 5 minutes
Serves: 4
Ingredients:
• 1 package Pillsbury Grands (Homestyle)
• ½ cup seedless raspberry jelly
• 1 tablespoon butter, melted
• ½ cup sugar
Preparation:
1. Install a crisper plate in both drawers. Place half of the biscuits in the zone 1 drawer and half in zone 2's, then insert the drawers into the unit. You may need to cook in batches.
2. Select zone 1, select AIR FRY, set temperature to 390°F, and set time to 22 minutes. Select MATCH to match zone 2 settings to zone 1. Press the START/STOP button to begin cooking.
3. Place the sugar into a wide bowl with a flat bottom.
4. Baste all sides of the cooked biscuits with the melted butter and roll in the sugar to cover completely.
5. Using a long cake tip, pipe 1–2 tablespoons of raspberry jelly into each biscuit. You've now got raspberry-filled donuts!
Serving Suggestion: Serve with your favorite hot beverage.
Variation Tip: You can use brown sugar instead.
Nutritional Information Per Serving:
Calories 252 | Fat 7g | Sodium 503mg | Carbs 45g | Fiber 0g | Sugar 23g | Protein 3g

Conclusion

All the MYTHS have gone, as this cookbook help, you prepared a wide variety of meals using an air fryer.

No doubt once you buy this appliance you will surely be impressed by its usefulness and wide cooking functionality.

Moreover, this cookbook is written in a very exciting yet easy tone, so that as a beginner you can prepare some delicious homemade recipes

The recipe collection is versatile and packed with flavor and nutrition. The ingredients are not expensive and are available at the local stores. Hopefully, in the end, the users can fulfill their aim of creating new recipes using an air fryer, as it improves the overall experience of cooking because of its preset button and quick heating technology.

The recipes prepare in an air fryer are loaded with nutrition and are less in fat. We highly recommend buying it for you.

Appendix 1 Measurement Conversion Chart

WEIGHT EQUIVALENTS

US STANDARD	METRIC (APPROXINATE)
1 ounce	28 g
2 ounces	57 g
5 ounces	142 g
10 ounces	284 g
15 ounces	425 g
16 ounces (1 pound)	455 g
1.5pounds	680 g
2pounds	907 g

VOLUME EQUIVALENTS (LIQUID)

US STANDARD	US STANDARD (OUNCES)	METRIC (APPROXIMATE)
2 tablespoons	1 fl.oz	30 mL
¼ cup	2 fl.oz	60 mL
½ cup	4 fl.oz	120 mL
1 cup	8 fl.oz	240 mL
1½ cup	12 fl.oz	355 mL
2 cups or 1 pint	16 fl.oz	475 mL
4 cups or 1 quart	32 fl.oz	1 L
1 gallon	128 fl.oz	4 L

VOLUME EQUIVALENTS (DRY)

US STANDARD	METRIC (APPROXIMATE)
⅛ teaspoon	0.5 mL
¼ teaspoon	1 mL
½ teaspoon	2 mL
¾ teaspoon	4 mL
1 teaspoon	5 mL
1 tablespoon	15 mL
¼ cup	59 mL
½ cup	118 mL
¾ cup	177 mL
1 cup	235 mL
2 cups	475 mL
3 cups	700 mL
4 cups	1 L

TEMPERATURES EQUIVALENTS

FAHRENHEIT(F)	CELSIUS(C) (APPROXIMATE)
225 °F	107 °C
250 °F	120 °C
275 °F	135 °C
300 °F	150 °C
325 °F	160 °C
350 °F	180 °C
375 °F	190 °C
400 °F	205 °C
425 °F	220 °C
450 °F	235 °C
475 °F	245 °C
500 °F	260 °C

Appendix 2 Air Fryer Cooking Chart

Chicken	Temp(℉)	Time (min)
Chicken Whole (3.5 lbs)	350	45-60
Chicken Breast (boneless)	380	12-15
Chicken Breast (bone-in)	350	22-25
Chicken Drumsticks	380	23-25
Chicken Thighs (bone-in)	380	23-25
Chicken Tenders	350	8-12
Chicken Wings	380	22-25

Beef	Temp(℉)	Time (min)
Burgers (1/4 Pound)	350	8-12
Filet Mignon (4 oz.)	370	15-20
Flank Steak (1.5 lbs)	400	10-14
Meatballs (1 inch)	380	7-10
London Broil (2.5 lbs.)	400	22-28
Round Roast (4 lbs)	390	45-55
Sirloin Steak (12oz)	390	9-14

Pork & Lamb	Temp(℉)	Time
Bacon	350	8-12
Lamb Chops	400	8-12
Pork Chops (1" boneless)	400	8-10
Pork Loin (2 lbs.)	360	18-21
Rack of Lamb (24-32 oz.)	375	22-25
Ribs	400	10-15
Sausages	380	10-15

Fish & Seafood	Temp(℉)	Time
Calamari	400	4-5
Fish Fillets	400	10-12
Salmon Fillets	350	8-12
Scallops	400	5-7
Shrimp	370	5-7
Lobster Tails	370	5-7
Tuna Steaks	400	7-10

Vegetables	Temp(℉)	Time
Asparagus (1" slices)	400	5
Beets (whole)	400	40
Broccoli Florets	400	6
Brussel Sprouts (halved)	380	12-15
Carrots (1/2" slices)	360	12-15
Cauliflower Florets	400	10-12
Corn on the Cob	390	6-7
Eggplant (1 1/2" cubes)	400	12-15
Green Beans	400	4-6
Kale Leaves	250	12
Mushrooms (1/4" slices)	400	4-5
Onions (pearl)	400	10
Peppers (1" chunks)	380	8-15
Potatoes (whole)	400	30-40
Potatoes (wedges)	390	15-18
Potatoes (1" cubes)	390	12-15
Potatoes (baby, 1.5 lbs.)	400	15
Squash (1" cubes)	390	15
Sweet Potato (whole)	380	30-35
Tomatoes (cherry)	400	5
Zucchini (1/2" sticks)	400	10-12

Frozen Foods	Temp(℉)	Time
Breaded Shrimp	400	8-9
Chicken Burger	360	12
Chicken Nuggets	370	10-12
Chicken Strips	380	12-15
Corn Dogs	400	7-9
Fish Fillets (1-2 lbs.)	400	10-12
Fish Sticks	390	12-15
French Fries	380	12-17
Hash Brown Patties	380	10-12
Meatballs (1-inch)	350	10-12
Mozzarella Sticks (11 oz.)	400	8
Meat Pies (1-2 pies)	370	23-25
Mozzarella Sticks	390	7-9
Onion Rings	400	10-12
Pizza	390	5-10
Tater Tots	380	15-17

Appendix 3 Recipes Index

H

Ham Burger Patties 74
Hash Browns 16
Herb and Lemon Cauliflower 41
Honey Sriracha Mahi Mahi 44
Honey Teriyaki Tilapia 44
Honey-Cajun Chicken Thighs 55

J

Jalapeño Popper Chicken 29
Jelly Donuts 87
Jerk-Rubbed Pork Loin With Carrots and Sage 70
Juicy Pork Chops 68

K

Kale and Spinach Chips 35
Keto Baked Salmon with Pesto 51
Korean BBQ Beef 72

L

Lamb Chops With Dijon Garlic 69
Lava Cake 81
Lemon Pepper Salmon with Asparagus 51
Lemony Sweet Twists 80

M

Mac and Cheese Balls 26
Meatloaf 71
Mini Blueberry Pies 79
Mini Strawberry and Cream Pies 79
Mixed Air Fry Veggies 35
Mozzarella Sticks 23
Mushroom Roll-Ups 37

O

Oreo Rolls 84

P

Paprika Pork Chops 69
Parmesan Crush Chicken 28
Parmesan Pork Chops 71
Pepper Poppers 41
Peppered Asparagus 28
Perfect Cinnamon Toast 19
Pork Chops 68
Pumpkin Muffins 20
Pumpkin Muffins with Cinnamon 86

Q

Quinoa Patties 34

R

Ravioli 25
Roast Beef 76
Roasted Salmon and Parmesan Asparagus 47
Rosemary and Garlic Lamb Chops 76

S

Salmon Nuggets 43
Salmon with Broccoli and Cheese 45
Salmon with Coconut 50
Salmon with Green Beans 44
Sausage with Eggs 13
Scallops 48
Seafood Shrimp Omelet 47
Sesame Ginger Chicken 54
Short Ribs & Root Vegetables 73
Shrimp With Lemon and Pepper 52
Smoked Salmon 50
Spiced Chicken and Vegetables 54
Spicy Chicken 63
Spicy Chicken Tenders 23
Spicy Fish Fillet with Onion Rings 45
Spicy Lamb Chops 67
Steak Fajitas With Onions and Peppers 73
Steak in Air Fry 68
Strawberries and Walnuts Muffins 30
Strawberry Nutella Hand Pies 81
Stuffed Bell Peppers 24
Stuffed Mushrooms 29
Stuffed Tomatoes 35
Sweet and Spicy Carrots with Chicken Thighs 58
Sweet Bites 24
Sweet Potatoes Hash 15
Sweet Potatoes with Honey Butter 39

T

Tater Tots 28
Thai Chicken Meatballs 56
Tomahawk Steak 72
Two-Way Salmon 52

W

Whole Chicken 59

Y

Yellow Potatoes with Eggs 13
Yogurt Lamb Chops 75
Yummy Chicken Breasts 64

Z

Zucchini Chips 32
Zucchini with Stuffing 33

Made in the USA
Las Vegas, NV
06 December 2024

13468358R10055